ARISTOTLE

BY A. E. TAYLOR • REVISED EDITION

DOVER PUBLICATIONS, INC., N.Y.

Published in Canada by General Publishing Company, Ltd., 30 Lesmill Road, Don Mills, Toronto, Ontario.
Published in the United Kingdom by Constable and Company, Ltd., 10 Orange Street, London WC 2.

This Dover edition, first published in 1955, is an unabridged reprinting of the revised edition published in 1919. It has been completely reset and contains a new index especially compiled for this edition by Geoffrey Mott-Smith.

Standard Book Number: 486-20280-1
Library of Congress Catalog Card Number: 59-8986

Manufactured in the United States of America

Dover Publications, Inc.
180 Varick Street
New York, N.Y. 10014

TABLE OF CONTENTS

I   LIFE AND WORKS   5

II   THE CLASSIFICATION OF THE
SCIENCES: SCIENTIFIC METHOD   14

III   FIRST PHILOSOPHY   41

IV   PHYSICS   61

V   PRACTICAL PHILOSOPHY   88

INDEX   113

LIFE AND WORKS I

not commonly been the lot of philosophers, as it is of great poets, that their names should become household words. We should hardly call an Englishman well read if he had not heard the name of Sophocles or Molière. An educated man is expected to know at least who these great writers were, and to understand an allusion to the *Antigone* or *Le Misanthrope*. But we call a man well read if his mind is stored with the verse of poets and the prose of historians, even though he were ignorant of the fame of Descartes or Kant. Yet there are a few philosophers whose influence on thought and language has been so extensive that no one who reads can be ignorant of their names, and that every man who speaks the language of educated Europeans is constantly using their vocabulary. Among this few Aristotle holds not the lowest place. We have all heard of him, as we have all heard of Homer. He has left his impress so firmly on theology that many of the formulae of the Churches are unintelligible without acquaintance with his conception of the universe. If we are interested in the growth of modern science we shall readily discover for ourselves that some knowledge of Aristotelianism is necessary for the understanding of Bacon and Galileo and the other great anti-Aristotelians who created the "modern scientific" view of Nature. If we turn to the imaginative literature of the modern languages, Dante is a sealed book, and many a passage of Chaucer and Shakespeare and Milton is half un-meaning to us unless we are at home in the outlines of Aristotle's philosophy. And if we turn to ordinary language, we find that many of the familiar turns of modern speech cannot be fully understood without a knowledge of the doctrines they were first forged to express. An Englishman who speaks of the "golden mean" or of "liberal education," or contrasts the "matter" of a work of literature with its "form," or the "essential" features of a situation or a scheme of policy with its "accidents," or "theory" with "practice," is using words which derive their significance from the part they play in the vocabulary of Aristotle. The unambitious object of this little book is, then, to help the English reader to a better understanding of such familiar language and a fuller comprehension of much that he will find in Dante and Shakespeare and Bacon and Milton.

LIFE OF ARISTOTLE

The main facts of Aristotle's life may be briefly told. He was born in 385–4 B.C. at Stagirus, a little city of the Chalci-dic peninsula, still called, almost by its ancient name, Chalcis, and died at the age of sixty-two at Chalcis in Euboea. Thus he is a contemporary of Demosthenes, his manhood wit-nessed the struggle which ended in the establishment of the Macedonian monarchy as the dominant power in Hellas, and his later years the campaigns in which his pupil Alexan-der the Great overthrew the Persian Empire and carried Greek civilisation to the banks of the Jumna. In studying the constitutional theories of Aristotle, it is necessary to bear these facts in mind. They help to explain certain limitations of outlook which might otherwise appear strange in so great a man. It throws a great deal of light on the philosopher's intense conviction of the natural inferiority of the "barbarian" intellect and character to remember that he grew up in an outlying region where the "barbarian" was seen to disadvantage in the ordinary course of life. Hence the distinction between Greek and "barbarian" came to mean for him much what the "colour-line" does to an American brought up in a Southern State. So, again, when we are struck by his "provincialism," his apparent satisfaction with the ideal of a small self-contained city-state with a decently oligarchical government, a good system of public education, and no "social problems," but devoid alike of great traditions and far-reaching ambitions, we must remember that the philosopher himself belonged to just such a tiny community without a past and without a future. The Chalcidic cities had been first founded, as the name of the peninsula implies, as colonies from the town of Chalcis in Euboea; Corinth had also been prominent in establishing settlements in the same region. At the height of Athenian Imperial prosperity in the age of Pericles the district had fallen politically under Athenian control, but had been detached again from Athens, in the last years of the Archidamian war, by the genius of the great Spartan soldier and diplomat Brasidas. Early in the fourth century the Chalcidic cities had attempted to form themselves into an independent federation, but the movement had been put down by Sparta, and the cities had fallen under the control of the rising Macedonian monarchy, when Aristotle was a baby. A generation later, a double intrigue of the cities with Philip of Macedon and Athens failed of its effect, and the peninsula was finally incorporated with the Macedonian kingdom. It is also

7

important to note that the philosopher belonged by birth to a guild, the Asclepiadae, in which the medical profession was hereditary. His father Nicomachus was court physician to Amyntas III, the king for whose benefit the Spartans had put down the Chalcidic league. This early connection with medicine and with the rough-living Macedonian court largely explains both the predominantly biological cast of Aristotle's philosophical thought and the intense dislike of "princes" and courts to which he more than once gives expression. At the age of eighteen, in 367–6, Aristotle was sent to Athens for "higher" education in philosophy and science, and entered the famous Platonic Academy, where he remained as a member of the scientific group gathered round the master for twenty years, until Plato's death in 347–6.* For the three years immediately following Aristotle was in Asia Minor with his friend and fellow-student Hermeias, who had become by force of sheer capacity monarch of the city of Atarneus in Aeolis, and was maintaining himself with much energy against the Persian king. Pythias, the niece of Hermeias, became the philosopher's wife, and it seems that the marriage was happy. Examination of Aristotle's contributions to marine biology has shown that his knowledge of the subject is specially good for the Aeolic coast and the shores of the adjacent islands. This throws light on his occupations during his residence with Hermeias, and suggests that Plato had discerned the bent of his distinguished pupil's mind, and that his special share in the researches of the Academy had, like that of Speusippus, Plato's nephew and successor in the headship of the school, been largely of a biological kind. We also know that, presumably shortly after Plato's death, Aristotle had been

---

* It is perhaps significant that Aristotle's entry into the school fell in the year when Plato was absent on his political mission in Syracuse. Thus he probably did not get his first introduction to Platonism from the lips of Plato.

one of the group of disciples who published their notes of
their teacher's famous unpublished lecture *On the Good*. In
343 Hermeias was assassinated at the instigation of Persia;
Aristotle honoured his memory by a hymn setting forth the
godlikeness of virtue as illustrated by the life of his friend.
Aristotle now removed to the Macedonian court, where he
received the position of tutor to the Crown Prince, afterwards Alexander the Great, at this time (343 B.C.) a boy of
thirteen. The association of the great philosopher and the
great king as tutor and pupil has naturally struck the
imagination of later ages; even in Plutarch's *Life of Alexander*
we meet already with the full-blown legend of the influence
of Aristotle's philosophical speculations on Alexander. It is,
however, improbable that Aristotle's influence counted for
much in forming the character of Alexander. Aristotle's
dislike of monarchies and their accessories is written large on
many a page of his *Ethics* and *Politics*; the small self-contained
city-state with no political ambitions for which he reserves
his admiration would have seemed a mere relic of antiquity
to Philip and Alexander. The only piece of contemporary
evidence as to the relations between the master and the pupil
is a sentence in a letter to the young Alexander from the
Athenian publicist Isocrates, who maliciously congratulates
the prince on his preference for "rhetoric," the art of
efficient public speech, and his indifference to "logic-
choppers." How little sympathy Aristotle can have had with
his pupil's ambitions is shown by the fact that, though his
political theories must have been worked out during the
very years in which Alexander was revolutionising Hellen-
ism by the foundation of his world-empire, they contain no
allusion to so momentous a change in the social order. For
all that Aristotle tells us, Alexander might never have
existed, and the small city-state might have been the last
word of Hellenic political development. Hence it is probable

9

that the selection of Aristotle, who had not yet appeared before the world as an independent thinker, to take part in the education of the Crown Prince was due less to personal reputation than to the connection of his family with the court, taken together with his own position as a pupil of Plato, whose intervention in the public affairs of Sicily had caused the Academy to be regarded as the special home of scientific interest in politics and jurisprudence. It may be true that Alexander found time in the midst of his conquests to supply his old tutor with zoological specimens; it is as certain as such a thing can be that the ideals and characters of the two men were too different to allow of any intimate influence of either on the other.

When Alexander was suddenly called to the Macedonian throne by the murder of his father in 336 B.C., Aristotle's services were no longer needed; he returned to Athens and gave himself to purely scientific work. Just at this juncture the presidency of the Academy was vacant by the death of Speusippus, Aristotle's old associate in biological research. Possibly Aristotle thought himself injured when the school passed him over and elected Xenocrates of Chalcedon as its new president. At any rate, though he appears never to have wholly severed his connection with the Academy, in 335 he opened a rival institution in the Lyceum, or gymnasium attached to the temple of Apollo Lyceus, to which he was followed by some of the most distinguished members of the Academy. From the fact that his instruction was given in the *peripatos* or covered portico of the gymnasium the school has derived its name of Peripatetic. For the next twelve years he was occupied in the organisation of the school as an abode for the prosecution of speculation and research in every department of inquiry, and in the composition of numerous courses of lectures on scientific and philosophical questions. The chief difference in general character between the new school and the Academy is that while the scientific interests of the Platonists centred in mathematics, the main contributions of the Lyceum to science lay in the department of biology and history.

Towards the end of Alexander's life his attention was unfavourably directed on his old teacher. A relative of Aristotle named Callisthenes had attended Alexander in his campaigns as historiographer, and had provoked disfavour by his censure of the King's attempts to invest his semi-constitutional position towards his Hellenic subjects with the pomp of an Oriental despotism. The historian's independence proved fatal. He was accused of instigating an assassination plot among Alexander's pages, and hanged, or, as some said, thrown into a prison where he died before trial. Alexander is reported to have held Aristotle responsible for his relative's treason, and to have meditated revenge. If this is so, he was fortunately diverted from the commission of a crime by preoccupation with the invasion of India.

On the death of Alexander in 323 a brief but vigorous anti-Macedonian agitation broke out at Athens. Aristotle, from his Macedonian connections, naturally fell a victim, in spite of his want of sympathy with the ideals of Philip and Alexander. Like Socrates, he was indicted on the capital charge of "impiety," the pretext being that his poem on the death of Hermeias, written twenty years before, was a virtual deification of his friend. This was, however, only a pretext; the real offence was political, and lay in his connection with the Macedonian leader Antipater. As condemnation was certain, the philosopher anticipated it by withdrawing with his disciples to Chalcis, the mother city of his native Stagirus. Here he died in the following year, at the age of sixty-two or sixty-three.

The features of Aristotle, familiar to us from busts and intaglios, are handsome, but indicate refinement and acuteness rather than originality, an impression in keeping with what we should expect from a study of his writings. The anecdotes related of him reveal a kindly, affectionate character, and show little trace of the self-importance which appears in his works. His will, which has been preserved, exhibits the same traits in its references to his happy family life and its solicitous care for the future of his children and servants. He was twice married, first to Pythias, and secondly to a certain Herpyllis, by whom he left a son Nicomachus and a daughter. The "goodness" of Herpyllis to her husband is specially mentioned in the clauses of the will which make provision for her, while the warmth of the writer's feelings for Pythias is shown by the direction that her remains are to be placed in the same tomb with his own. The list of servants remembered and the bequests enumerated show the philosopher to have been in easier circumstances than Plato.

THE WORKS OF ARISTOTLE

The so-called works of Aristotle present us with a curious problem. When we turn from Plato to his pupil we seem to have passed into a different atmosphere. The *Discourses of Socrates* exhibit a prose style which is perhaps the most marvellous of all literary achievements. Nowhere else do we meet with quite the same combination of eloquence, imaginative splendour, incisive logic, and irresistible wit and humour. The manner of Aristotle is dry and formal. His language bristles with technicalities, makes little appeal to the emotions, disdains graces of style, and frequently defies the simplest rules of composition. Our surprise is all the greater that we find later writers of antiquity, such as Cicero, commending Aristotle for his copious and golden eloquence, a characteristic which is conspicuously wanting in the Aristotelian writings we possess. The explanation of the puzzle is, however, simple. Plato and Aristotle were at once what we should call professors and men of letters; both wrote works for general circulation, and both delivered courses of lectures to special students. But while Plato's lectures have perished, his books have come down to us. Aristotle's books have almost wholly been lost, but we possess many of his lectures. The "works" of Aristotle praised by Cicero for their eloquence were philosophical dialogues, and formed the model for Cicero's own compositions in this kind. None of them have survived, though some passages have been preserved in quotations by later writers. That our "works" are actually the MSS. of a lecturer posthumously edited by his pupils seems clear from external as well as from internal evidence. In one instance we have the advantage of a double recension. Aristotle's *Ethics* or *Discourses on Conduct* have come down to us in two forms—the so-called *Nicomachean Ethics*, a redaction by the philosopher's son, Nicomachus, preserving all the characteristics of an oral course of lectures; and a freer and more readable recast by a pupil, the mathematician Eudemus, known as the *Eudemian Ethics*. In recent years we have also recovered from the sands of Egypt what appears to be our one specimen of a "work" of Aristotle, intended to be read by the public at large, the essay on the Constitution of Athens. The style of this essay is easy, flowing, and popular, and shows that Aristotle could write well and gracefully when he thought fit.

13

THE CLASSIFICATION

OF THE SCIENCES:

SCIENTIFIC METHOD

II

as understood by Aristotle, may be said to be the organised
whole of disinterested knowledge, that is, knowledge which
we seek for the satisfaction which it carries with itself, and
not as a mere means to utilitarian ends. The impulse which
receives this satisfaction is curiosity or wonder, which
Aristotle regards as innate in man, though it does not get full
play until civilisation has advanced far enough to make
secure provision for the immediate material needs of life.
Human curiosity was naturally directed first to the outstanding "marvellous works" of the physical world, the
planets, the periodicity of their movements, the return of the
seasons, winds, thunder and lightning, and the like. Hence
the earliest Greek speculation was concerned with problems
of astronomy and meteorology. Then, as reflection developed, men speculated about geometrical figure and
number, the possibility of having assured knowledge at all,
the character of the common principles assumed in all
branches of study or of the special principles assumed in
some one branch, and thus philosophy has finally become
the disinterested study of every department of Being or
Reality. Since Aristotle, like Hegel, thought that his own

doctrine was, in essentials, the last word of speculation, the complete expression of the principles by which his predecessors had been unconsciously guided, he believes himself in a position to make a final classification of the branches of science, showing how they are related and how they are discriminated from one another. This classification we have now to consider.

CLASSIFICATION OF THE SCIENCES

To begin with, we have to discriminate Philosophy from two rivals with which it might be confounded on a superficial view, Dialectic and Sophistry. Dialectic is the art of reasoning accurately from given premises, true or false. This art has its proper uses, and of one of these we shall have to speak. But in itself it is indifferent to the truth of its premisses. You may reason dialectically from premisses which you believe to be false, for the express purpose of showing the absurd conclusions to which they lead. Or you may reason from premisses which you assume tentatively to see what conclusions you are committed to if you adopt them. In either case your object is not directly to secure truth, but only to secure consistency. Science or Philosophy aims directly at *truth*, and hence requires to start with true and certain premisses. Thus the distinction between Science and Dialectic is that Science reasons from true premises, Dialectic only from "probable" or "plausible" premisses.* Sophistry differs from Science in virtue of its moral character. It is the profession of making a living by the abuse of reasoning, the trick of employing logical skill for the

---

* A proposition is regarded as "probable" if it is held either (1) by the great majority of men, or (2) by one or more men of special eminence in a subject. This is the ultimate origin of the "Probabilism" of "moral theologians."

15

apparent demonstration of scientific or ethical falsehoods. "The sophist is one who earns a living from an apparent but unreal wisdom." (The emphasis thus falls on the notion of making an "unreal wisdom" into a *trade*. The sophist's real concern is to get his fee.) Science or Philosophy is thus the disinterested employment of the understanding in the discovery of truth.

We may now distinguish the different branches of science as defined. The first and most important division to be made is that between Speculative or Theoretical Science and Practical Science. The broad distinction is that which we should now draw between the Sciences and the Arts (*i.e.* the industrial and technical, not the "fine" arts). Speculative or Theoretical Philosophy differs from Practical Philosophy in its purpose, and, in consequence, in its subject-matter, and its formal logical character. The purpose of the former is the disinterested contemplation of truths which are what they are independently of our own volition; its end is to *know* and only to know. The object of "practical" Science is to know, but not only to know but also to turn our knowledge to account in devising ways of successful interference with the course of events. (The real importance of the distinction comes out in Aristotle's treatment of the problems of moral and social science. Since we require knowledge of the moral and social nature of men not merely to satisfy an intellectual interest, but as a basis for a sound system of education and government, Politics, the theory of government, and Ethics, the theory of goodness of conduct, which for Aristotle is only a subordinate branch of Politics, belong to Practical, not to Theoretical Philosophy, a view which is attended by important consequences.)

It follows that there is a corresponding difference in the objects investigated by the two branches of Philosophy. Speculative or Theoretical Philosophy is concerned with "that which cannot possibly be other than it is," truths and relations independent of human volition for their subsistence, and calling simply for *recognition* on our part. Practical Philosophy has to do with relations which human volition can modify, "things which may be other than they are," the contingent. (Thus *e.g.* not only politics, but medicine and economics will belong to Practical Science.)

Hence again arises a logical difference between the conclusions of Theoretical and those of Practical Philosophy. Those of the former are universal truths deducible with logical necessity from self-evident* principles. Those of the latter, because they relate to what "can be otherwise," are never rigidly universal; they are *general* rules which hold good "in the majority of cases," but are liable to occasional exceptions owing to the contingent character of the facts with which they deal. It is a proof of a philosopher's lack of grounding in logic that he looks to the results of a practical science (*e.g.* to the detailed precepts of medicine or ethics) for a higher degree of certainty and validity than the nature of the subject-matter allows. Thus for Aristotle the distinction between the necessary and the contingent is real and not merely apparent, and "probability is the guide" in studies which have to do with the direction of life.

We proceed to the question how many subdivisions there are within "theoretical" Philosophy itself. Plato had held that there are none. All the sciences are deductions from a single set of ultimate principles which it is the business of that supreme science to which Plato had given the name of Dialectic to establish. This is not Aristotle's view. According to him, "theoretical" Philosophy falls into a number of dis-

---

* Self-evident, that is, in a purely logical sense. When you apprehend the principles in question, you *see* at once that they are true, and do not require to have them *proved*. It is not meant that any and every man *does*, in point of fact, always apprehend the principles, or that they can be apprehended without preliminary mental discipline.

tinct though not co-ordinate branches, each with its own special subjects of investigation and its own special axiomatic principles. Of these branches there are three, First Philosophy, Mathematics, and Physics. First Philosophy—afterwards to be known to the Middle Ages as Metaphysics★—treats, to use Aristotle's own expression, of "Being quà Being." This means that it is concerned with the universal characteristics which belong to the system of knowable reality as such, and the principles of its organisation in their full universality. First Philosophy alone investigates the character of those causative factors in the system which are without body or shape and exempt from all mutability. Since in Aristotle's system God is the supreme Cause of this kind, First Philosophy culminates in the knowledge of God, and is hence frequently called Theology. It thus includes an element which would to-day be assigned to the theory of knowledge, as well as one which we should ascribe to metaphysics, since it deals at once with the ultimate postulates of knowledge and the ultimate causes of the order of real existence.

Mathematics is of narrower scope. What it studies is no longer "real being as such," but only real being in so far as it exhibits number and geometrical form. Since Aristotle holds the view that number and figure only exist as determinations of objects given in perception (though by a convenient fiction the mathematician treats of them in abstraction from the perceived objects which they qualify), he marks the difference between Mathematics and First Philosophy by saying that "whereas the objects of First Philosophy are separate from matter and devoid of motion, those of Mathe-

★ The origin of this name seems to be that Aristotle's lectures on First Philosophy came to be studied as a continuation of his course on Physics. Hence the lectures got the name *Metaphysica* because they came *after* (*meta*) those on Physics. Finally the name was transferred (as in the case of *Ethics*) from the lectures to the subject of which they treat.

matics, though incapable of motion, have no separable existence but are inherent in matter." Physics is concerned with the study of objects which are both material and capable of motion. Thus the principle of the distinction is the presence or absence of initial restrictions of the range of the different branches of Science. First Philosophy has the widest range, since its contemplation covers the whole ground of the real and knowable; Physics the narrowest, because it is confined to a "universe of discourse" restricted by the double qualification that its members are all material and capable of displacement. Mathematics holds an intermediate position, since in it one of these qualifications is removed, but the other still remains, for the geometer's figures are boundaries and limits of sensible bodies, and the arithmetician's numbers properties of collections of concrete objects. It follows also that the initial axioms or postulates of Mathematics form a less simple system than those of First Philosophy, and those of Physics than those of Mathematics. Mathematics requires as initial assumptions not only those which hold good for *all* thought, but certain other special axioms which are only valid and significant for the realm of figure and number; Physics requires yet further axioms which are only applicable to "what is in motion." This is why, though the three disciplines are treated as distinct, they are not strictly co-ordinate, and "First Philosophy," though "first," is only *prima inter pares*.

We thus get the following diagrammatic scheme of the classification of sciences:—

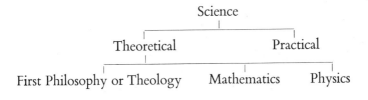

Science

Theoretical   Practical

First Philosophy or Theology   Mathematics   Physics

Practical Philosophy is not subjected by Aristotle to any similar subdivision. Later students were accustomed to recognise a threefold division into Ethics (the theory of individual conduct), Economics (the theory of the management of the household), Politics (the theory of the management of the State). Aristotle himself does not make these distinctions. His general name for the theory of conduct is Politics, the doctrine of individual conduct being for him inseparable from that of the right ordering of society. Though he composed a separate course of lectures on individual conduct (the *Ethics*), he takes care to open the course by stating that the science of which it treats is Politics, and offers an apology for dealing with the education of individual character apart from the more general doctrine of the organisation of society. No special recognition is given in Aristotle's own classification to the Philosophy of Art. Modern students of Aristotle have tried to fill in the omission by adding artistic creation to contemplation and practice as a third fundamental form of mental activity, and thus making a threefold division of Philosophy into Theoretical, Practical, and Productive. The object of this is to find a place in the classification for Aristotle's famous *Poetics* and his work on *Rhetoric*, the art of effective speech and writing. But the admission of the third division of Science has no warrant in the text of Aristotle, nor are the *Rhetoric* and *Poetics*, properly speaking, a contribution to Philosophy. They are intended as collections of practical rules for the composition of a pamphlet or a tragedy, not as a critical examination of the canons of literary taste. This was correctly seen by the dramatic theorists of the seventeenth century. They exaggerated the value of Aristotle's directions and entirely misunderstood the meaning of some of them, but they were right in their view that the *Poetics* was meant to be a collection of rules by obeying which the craftsman might make sure of turning out a

successful play. So far as Aristotle has a Philosc
Art at all, it forms part of his more general thec
tion and must be looked for in the general disc
aims of education contained in his *Politics*.

THE METHODS OF SCIENCE

No place has been assigned in the scheme to what we call
logic and Aristotle called *Analytics*, the theory of scientific
method, or of proof and the estimation of evidence. The
reason is that since the fundamental character of proof is the
same in all science, Aristotle looks upon logic as a study of
the methods common to all science. At a later date it became a hotly debated question whether logic should be
regarded in this way as a study of the methods instrumental
to proof in all sciences, or as itself a special constituent
division of philosophy. The Aristotelian view was concisely
indicated by the name which became attached to the collection of Aristotle's logical works. They were called the
Organon, that is, the "instrument," or the body of rules of
method employed by Science. The thought implied is thus
that logic furnishes the *tools* with which every science has
to work in establishing its results. Our space will only permit
of a brief statement as to the points in which the Aristotelian
formal logic appears to be really original, and the main
peculiarities of Aristotle's theory of knowledge.

FORMAL LOGIC

In compass the Aristotelian logic corresponds roughly with
the contents of modern elementary treatises on the same
subject, with the omission of the sections which deal with

the so-called Conditional Syllogism. The inclusion of arguments of this type in mediaeval and modern expositions of formal logic is principally due to the Stoics, who preferred to throw their reasoning into these forms and subjected them to minute scrutiny. In his treatment of the doctrine of Terms, Aristotle avoids the mistake of treating the isolated name as though it had significance apart from the enunciations in which it occurs. He is quite clear on the all-important point that the unit of thought is the proposition in which something is affirmed or denied, the one thought-form which can be properly called "true" or "false." Such an assertion he analyses into two factors, that about which something is affirmed or denied (the Subject), and that which is affirmed or denied of it (the Predicate). Consequently his doctrine of the classification of Terms is based on a classification of Predicates, or of Propositions according to the special kind of connection between the Subject and Predicate which they affirm or deny. Two such classifications, which cannot be made to fit into one another, meet us in Aristotle's logical writings, the scheme of the ten "Categories" or "Predicaments," and that which was afterwards known in the Middle Ages as the list of "Predicables," or again as the "Five Words." The list of "Categories" reveals itself as an attempt to answer the question in how many different senses the words "is a" or "are" are employed when we assert that "x is y" or "x is a y" or "xs are ys." Such a statement may tell us (1) what x is, as if I say "x is a lion"; the predicate is then said to fall under the category of Substance; (2) what x like, as when I say "x is white, or x is wise,"—the category of Quality; (3) how much or how many x is, as when I say "there are five xs" or "x is five feet long,"—the category of Quantity; (4) how x is related to something else, as when I say "x is to the right of y," "x is the father of y,"—the category of Relation. These are the four chief "categories" discussed by Aristotle. The remainder are (5) Place, (6) Time, (7) and (8) Condition or State, as when I say "x is sitting down" or "x has his armour on,"—(the only distinction between the two cases seems to be that (7) denotes a more permanent state of x than (8)); (9) Action or Activity, as when I say "x is cutting," or generally "x is doing something to y"; (10) Passivity, as when I say "x is being cut," or more generally, "so-and-so is being done to x." No attempt is made to show that this list of "figures of predication" is complete, or to point out any principle which has been followed in its construction. It also happens that much the same enumeration is incidentally made in one or two passages of Plato. Hence it is not unlikely that the list was taken over by Aristotle as one which would be familiar to pupils who had read their Plato, and therefore convenient for practical purposes. The *fivefold* classification does depend on a principle pointed out by Aristotle which guarantees its completeness, and is therefore likely to have been thought out by him for himself, and to be the genuine Aristotelian scheme. Consider an ordinary universal affirmative proposition of the form "all xs are ys." Now if this statement is true it may also be true that "all ys are xs," or it may not. On the first supposition we have two possible cases, (1) the predicate may state precisely what the subject defined *is*; then y is the Definition of x, as when I say that "men are mortal animals, capable of discourse." Here it is also true to say that "mortal animals capable of discourse are men," and Aristotle regards the predicate "mortal animal capable of discourse" as expressing the inmost nature of man. (2) The predicate may not express the inmost nature of the subject, and yet may belong only to the class denoted by the subject and to every member of that class. The predicate is then called a Proprium or property, an exclusive attribute of the class in question. Thus it was held that "all men are capable of laughter" and "all beings capable of laughter are men," but that the capacity for laughter is no part of the inmost nature or "real essence" of humanity. It is therefore reckoned as a Proprium.

Again in the case where it is true that "all xs are ys," but not true that all "ys are xs," y may be part of the definition of x or it may not. If it is part of the definition of x it will be either (3) a Genus or wider class of which x forms a sub-division, as when I say, "All men are animals," or (4) a Difference, that is, one of the distinctive marks by which the xs are distinguished from other sub-classes or species of the same genus, as when I say, "All men are capable of discourse." Or finally (5) y may be no part of the definition of x, but a characteristic which belongs both to the xs and some things other than xs. The predicate is then called an Accident. We have now exhausted all the possible cases, and may say that the predicate of a universal affirmative proposition is always either a definition, a proprium, a genus, a difference, or an accident. This classification reached the Middle Ages not in the precise form in which it is given by Aristotle, but with modifications mainly due to the Neo-Platonic philosopher Porphyry. In its modified form it is regarded as a classification of terms generally. Definition disappears from the list, as the definition is regarded as a complex made up of the genus, or next highest class to which the class to be defined belongs, and the differences which mark off this particular species or sub-class. The species itself which figures as the subject-term in a definition is added, and thus the "Five Words" of mediaeval logic are enumerated as genus, species, difference, proprium, accident.

The one point of philosophical interest about this doctrine appears alike in the scheme of the "Categories" in the presence of a category of "substance," and in the list of "Predicables" in the sharp distinction drawn between "definition" and "proprium." From a logical point of view it does not appear why *any* proprium, *any* character belonging to all the members of a class and to them alone, should not be taken as defining the class. Why should it be assumed that there is only *one* predicate, viz. *man*, which precisely answers the question, "What is Socrates?" Why should it not be equally correct to answer, "a Greek," or "a philosopher"? The explanation is that Aristotle takes it for granted that not all the distinctions we can make between "kinds" of things are arbitrary and subjective. Nature herself has made certain hard and fast divisions between kinds which it is the business of our thought to recognise and follow. Thus according to Aristotle there is a real gulf, a genuine difference in kind, between the horse and the ass, and this is illustrated by the fact that the mule, the offspring of a horse and an ass, is not capable of propagating. It is thus a sort of imperfect being, a kind of "monster" existing *contra naturam*. Such differences as we find when we compare *e.g.* Egyptians with Greeks do not amount to a difference in "kind." To say that Socrates is a man tells me what Socrates *is*, because the statement places Socrates in the real kind to which he actually belongs; to say that he is wise, or old, or a philosopher merely tells me some of his attributes. It follows from this belief in "real" or "natural" kinds that the problem of definition acquires an enormous importance for science. We, who are accustomed to regard the whole business of classification as a matter of making a grouping of our materials such as is most pertinent to the special question we have in hand, tend to look upon any predicate which belongs universally and exclusively to the members of a group, as a sufficient basis for a possible definition of the group. Hence we are prone to take the "nominalist" view of definition, *i.e.* to look upon a definition as no more than a declaration of the sense which we intend henceforward to

25

put on a word or other symbol.* And consequently we readily admit that there may be as many definitions of a class as it has different propria. But in a philosophy like that of Aristotle, in which it is held that a true classification must not only be formally satisfactory, but must also conform to the actual lines of cleavage which Nature has established between kind and kind, and task of classificatory science becomes much more difficult. Science is called on to supply not merely *a* definition but *the* definition of the classes it considers, *the* definition which faithfully reflects the "lines of cleavage" in Nature. This is why the Aristotelian view is that a true definition should always be *per genus et differentias*. It should "place" a given class by mentioning the wider class next above it in the objective hierarchy, and then enumerating the most deep-seated distinctions by which Nature herself marks off this class from others belonging to the same wider class. Modern evolutionary thought may possibly bring us back to this Aristotelian standpoint. Modern evolutionary science differs from Aristotelianism on one point of the first importance. It regards the difference between kinds, not as a primary fact of Nature, but as produced by a long process of accumulation of slight differences. But a world in which the process has progressed far enough will exhibit much the same character as the Nature of Aristotle. As the intermediate links between "species" drop out because they are less thoroughly adapted to maintain themselves than the extremes between which they form links, the world produced approximates more and more to a system of species between which there are unbridgeable chasms; evolution tends more and more to the final establishment of "real kinds," marked by the fact

---

* All mathematical definitions are of this kind, and are thus purely "nominal."

that there is no permanent possibility of cross-breeding between them. This makes it once more possible to distinguish between a "nominal" definition and a "real" definition. From an evolutionary point of view, a "real" definition would be one which specifies not merely enough characters to mark off the group defined from others, but selects also for the purpose those characters which indicate the line of historical development by which the group has successively separated itself from other groups descended from the same ancestors. We shall learn yet more of the significance of this conception of a "real kind" as we go on to make acquaintance with the outlines of First Philosophy. Over the rest of the formal logic of Aristotle we must be content to pass more rapidly. In connection with the doctrine of Propositions, Aristotle lays down the familiar distinction between the four types of proposition according to their quantity (as universal or particular) and quality (as affirmative or negative), and treats of their contrary and contradictory opposition in a way which still forms the basis of the handling of the subject in elementary works on formal logic. He also considers at great length a subject nowadays commonly excluded from the elementary books—the modal distinction between the Problematic proposition (x may be y), the Assertory (x is y), and the Necessary (x must be y), and the way in which all these forms may be contradicted. For him, modality is a formal distinction like quantity or quality, because he believes that contingency and necessity are not merely relative to the state of our knowledge, but represent real and objective features of the order of Nature.

In connection with the doctrine of Inference, it is worth while to give his definition of Syllogism or Inference (literally "computation") in his own words. "Syllogism is a discourse wherein certain things (viz. the premisses) being admitted, something else, different from what has been admitted, follows of necessity because the admissions are what they are." The last clause shows that Aristotle is aware that the all-important thing in an inference is not that the conclusion should be novel but that it should be proved. We may have known the conclusion as a fact before; what the inference does for us is to connect it with the rest of our knowledge, and thus to show *why* it is true. He also formulates the axiom upon which syllogistic inference rests, that "if A is predicated universally of B and B of C, A is necessarily predicated universally of C." Stated in the language of class-inclusion, and adapted to include the case where B is denied of C, this becomes the formula, "whatever is asserted universally, whether positively or negatively, of a class B is asserted in like manner of any class C which is wholly contained in B," the axiom *de omni et nullo* of mediaeval logic. The syllogism of the "first figure," to which this principle immediately applies, is accordingly regarded by Aristotle as the natural and perfect form of inference. Syllogisms of the second and third figures can only be shown to fall under the dictum by a process of "reduction" or transformation into corresponding arguments in the first "figure," and are therefore called "imperfect" or "incomplete," because they do not exhibit the conclusive force of the reasoning with equal clearness, and also because no universal affirmative conclusion can be proved in them, and the aim of science is always to establish such affirmatives. The list of "moods" of the three figures, and the doctrine of the methods by which each mood of the imperfect figures can be replaced by an equivalent mood of the first, is worked out substantially as in our current text-books. The so-called "fourth" figure is not recognised, its moods being regarded merely as unnatural and distorted statements of those of the first figure.

INDUCTION

Of the use of "induction" in Aristotle's philosophy we shall speak under the head of "Theory of Knowledge." Formally it is called "the way of proceeding from particular facts to universals," and Aristotle insists that the conclusion is only proved if *all* the particulars have been examined. Thus he gives as an example the following argument: "x, y, z are long-lived species of animals; x, y, z are the only species which have no gall; *ergo* all animals which have no gall are long-lived." This is the "induction by simple enumeration" denounced by Francis Bacon on the ground that it may always be discredited by the production of a single "contrary instance"—*e.g.* a single instance of an animal which has no gall and yet is not long-lived. Aristotle is quite aware that his "induction" does not establish its conclusion unless all the cases have been included in the examination. In fact, as his own example shows, an induction which gives certainty does not start with "particular facts" at all. It is a method of arguing that what has been proved true of each sub-class of a wider class will be true of the wider class as a whole. The premisses are strictly universal throughout. In general, Aristotle does not regard "induction" as *proof* at all. Historically "induction" is held by Aristotle to have been first made prominent in philosophy by Socrates, who constantly employed the method in his attempts to elicit universal results in moral science. Thus he gives, as a characteristic argument for the famous Socratic doctrine that knowledge is the one thing needful, the "induction," "he who understands the theory of navigation is the best navigator, he who understands the theory of chariot-driving the best driver; from these examples we see that universally he who understands the theory of a thing is the best practitioner," where it is evident that *all* the relevant cases have *not* been examined, and consequently that the reasoning does not amount to proof. Mill's so-called reasoning from particulars to particulars finds a place in Aristotle's theory under the name of "arguing from an example." He gives as an illustration, "A war between Athens and Thebes will be a bad thing, for we see that the war between Thebes and Phocis was so." He is careful to point out that the whole force of the argument depends on the *implied* assumption of a universal proposition which covers both cases, such as "wars between *neighbours* are bad things." Hence he calls such appeals to example "rhetorical" reasoning, because the politician★ is accustomed to leave his hearers to supply the relevant universal consideration for themselves.

THEORY OF KNOWLEDGE

Here, as everywhere in Aristotle's philosophy, we are confronted by an initial and insuperable difficulty. Aristotle is always anxious to insist on the difference between his own doctrines and those of Plato, and his bias in this direction regularly leads him to speak as though he held a thoroughgoing naturalistic and empirical theory with no "transcendental moonshine" about it. Yet his final conclusions on all points of importance are hardly distinguishable from those of Plato, except by the fact that, as they are so much at variance with the naturalistic side of his philosophy, they have the appearance of being sudden lapses into an alogical mysticism. We shall find the presence of this "fault" more pronouncedly in his metaphysics, psychology, and ethics than in his theory of knowledge, but it is not absent from any part of his philosophy. He is everywhere a Platonist

★ We must remember that "rhetorician" or "orator," in the Greek of Aristotle's day, means "politician."

malgré lui, and it is just the Platonic element in his thought to which it owes its hold over men's minds.

Plato's doctrine on the subject may be stated with enough accuracy for our purpose as follows. There is a radical distinction between sense-perception and scientific knowledge. A scientific truth is exact and definite, it is also true once and for all, and never becomes truer or falser with the lapse of time. This is the character of the propositions of the science which Plato regarded as the type of what true science ought to be—pure mathematics. It is very different with the judgments which we try to base on our sense-perceptions of the visible and tangible world. The colours, tastes, shapes of sensible things seem different to different percipients, and moreover they are constantly changing in incalculable ways. We can never be certain that two lines which seem to our senses to be equal are really so; it may be that the inequality is merely too slight to be perceptible to our senses. No figure which we can draw and see actually has the exact properties ascribed by the mathematician to a circle or a square. Hence Plato concludes that if the word science be taken in its fullest sense, there can be no science about the world which our senses reveal. We can have only an approximate knowledge, a knowledge which is after all, at best, probable opinion. The objects of which the mathematician has certain, exact, and final knowledge cannot be anything which the senses reveal. They are objects of *thought*, and the function of visible models and diagrams in mathematics is not to present *examples* of them to us, but only to show us imperfect *approximations* to them, and so to "remind" the soul of objects and relations between them which she has never cognised with the bodily senses. Thus mathematical straightness is never actually beheld, but when we see lines of less and more approximate straightness we are "put in mind" of that absolute straightness to which sense-perception only approximates. So in the moral sciences, the various "virtues" are not presented in their perfection by the course of daily life. We do not meet with men who are perfectly brave or just, but the experience that one man is braver or juster than another "calls into our mind" the thought of the absolute standard of courage or justice implied in the conviction that one man comes nearer to it than another, and it is these absolute standards which are the real objects of our attention when we try to define the terms by which we describe the moral life. This is the "epistemological" side of the famous doctrine of the "Ideas." The main points are two: (1) that strict science deals throughout with objects and relations between objects which are of a purely intellectual or conceptual order, no sense-data entering into their constitution; (2) since the objects of science are of this character, it follows that the "Idea" or "concept" or "universal" is not arrived at by any process of "abstracting" from our experience of sensible things the features common to them all. As the particular fact never actually exhibits the "universal" except approximately, the "universal" cannot be simply disentangled from particulars by abstraction. As Plato puts it, it is "apart from" particulars, or, as we might reword his thought, the pure concepts of science represent "upper limits" to which the comparative series which we can form out of sensible data continually approximate but do not reach them.

In his theory of knowledge Aristotle begins by brushing aside the Platonic view. Science requires no such "Ideas," transcending sense-experience, as Plato had spoken of; they are, in fact, no more than "poetic metaphors." What is required for science is not that there should be a "one over and above the many" (that is, such pure concepts, unrealised in the world of actual perception, as Plato had spoken of), but only that it should be possible to predicate one term universally of many others. This, by itself, means that the "universal" is looked on as a mere residue of the characteristics found in each member of a group, got by abstraction—*i.e.* by leaving out of view the characteristics which are peculiar to some of the group and retaining only those which are common to all. If Aristotle had held consistently to this point of view, his theory of knowledge would have been a purely empirical one. He would have had to say that, since all the objects of knowledge are particular facts given in sense-perception, the universal laws of science are a mere convenient way of describing the observed uniformities in the behaviour of sensible things. But since it is obvious that in pure mathematics we are not concerned with the actual relations between sensible data or the actual ways in which they behave, but with so-called "pure cases" or ideals to which the perceived world only approximately conforms, he would also have had to say that the propositions of mathematics are not strictly true. In modern times consistent empiricists have said this, but it is not a position possible to one who had passed twenty years in association with the mathematicians of the Academy, and Aristotle's theory only begins in naturalism to end in Platonism. We may condense its most ·striking positions into the following statement. By science we mean *proved* knowledge. And proved knowledge is always "mediated"; it is the knowledge of *conclusions* from premisses. A truth that is scientifically known does not stand alone. The "proof" is simply the pointing out of the connection between the truth we call the conclusion and other truths which we call the premisses of our demonstration. Science points out the *reason why* of things, and this is what is meant by the Aristotelian principle that to have science is to know things through their *causes* or *reasons why*. In an ordered digest of scientific truths, the proper arrangement is to begin with the simplest and most widely extended principles and to reason down, through successive inferences, to the most complex propositions, the *reason why* of which can only be exhibited by long chains of deductions. This is the order of logical dependence, and is described by Aristotle as reasoning *from* what is "more knowable in its own nature,"* the simple, to what is usually "more familiar to *us*," because less removed from the infinite wealth of sense-perception, the complex. In *discovery* we have usually to reverse the process and argue from "the familiar to us," highly complex facts, to "the more knowable in its own nature," the simpler principles implied in the facts.

It follows that Aristotle, after all, admits the disparateness of sense-perception and scientific knowledge. Sense perception of itself never gives us scientific truth, because it can only assure us that a fact is so; it cannot *explain* the fact by showing its connection with the rest of the system of facts, "it does not give the *reason* for the fact." Knowledge of perception is always "immediate," and for that very reason is never scientific. If we stood on the moon and saw the earth interposing between us and the sun, we should still not have scientific knowledge about the eclipse, because "we should still have to ask for the *reason why*." (In fact, we should not know the reason *why* without a theory of light including the proposition that light-waves are propagated in straight lines and several others.) Similarly Aristotle insists that Induction does not yield scientific proof. "He who makes an induction points out something, but does not demonstrate anything."

For instance, if we know that *each* species of animal which is without a gall is long-lived, we may make the induction that *all* animals without a gall are long-lived, but in doing so we have got no nearer to seeing *why* or *how* the absence of a gall makes for longevity. The questions which we may raise

* This simple expression acquires a mysterious appearance in mediaeval philosophy from the standing mistranslation *notiora naturae*, "better known *to* nature."

in science may all be reduced to four heads: (1) Does this thing exist? (2) Does this event occur? (3) If the thing exists, precisely *what* is it? and (4) If the event occurs, *why* does it occur? and science has not completed its task unless it can advance from the solution of the first two questions to that of the latter two. Science is no mere catalogue of things and events; it consists of inquiries into the "real essences" and characteristics of things and the laws of connection between events.

Looking at scientific reasoning, then, from the point of view of its formal character, we may say that all science consists in the search for "middle terms" of syllogisms, by which to connect the truth which appears as a conclusion with the less complex truths which appear as the premisses from which it is drawn. When we ask, "does such a thing exist?" or "does such an event happen?" we are asking, "is there a middle term which can connect the thing or event in question with the rest of known reality?" Since it is a rule of the syllogism that the middle term must be taken universally, at least once in the premisses, the search for middle terms may also be described as the search for universals, and we may speak of science as knowledge of the universal interconnections between facts and events.

A science, then, may be analysed into three constituents. These are: (1) A determinate class of objects which form the subject-matter of its inquiries. In an orderly exhibition of the contents of the science, these appear, as in Euclid, as the initial data about which the science reasons. (2) A number of principles, postulates, and axioms, from which our demonstrations must start. Some of these will be principles employed in all scientific reasoning; others will be specific to the subject-matter with which a particular science is concerned. (3) Certain characteristics of the objects under study which can be shown by means of our axioms and postulates to follow from our initial definitions, the *accidentia per se* of the objects defined. It is these last which are expressed by the conclusions of scientific demonstration. We are said to know scientifically that B is true of A when we show that this follows, in virtue of the principles of some science, from the initial definition of A. Thus if we convinced ourselves that the sum of the angles of a plane triangle is equal to two right angles by measurement, we could not be said to have scientific knowledge of the proposition. But if we show that the same proposition follows from the definition of a plane triangle by repeated applications of admitted axioms or postulates of geometry, our knowledge is genuinely scientific. We now know that it is so, and we see *why* it is so; we see the connection of this truth with the simple initial truths of geometry.

This leads us to the consideration of the most characteristic point of Aristotle's whole theory. Science is demonstrated knowledge—that is, it is the knowledge that certain truths follow from still simpler truths. Hence the simplest of all the truths of any science cannot themselves be capable of being known by inference. You cannot infer that the axioms of geometry are true because its conclusions are true, since the truth of the conclusions is itself a consequence of the truth of the axioms. Nor yet must you ask for demonstration of the axioms as consequences of still simpler premisses, because if all truths can be proved, they ought to be proved, and you would therefore require an infinity of successive demonstrations to prove anything whatever. But under such conditions all knowledge of demonstrated truth would be impossible. The first principles of any science must therefore be indemonstrable. They must be known, as facts of sense-perception are known, immediately and not mediately. How then do we come by our knowledge of them? Aristotle's answer to this question appears at first sight curiously contradictory. He seems to say that these simplest truths are apprehended intuitively, or on inspection, as self-evident by Intelligence or Mind. On the other hand, he also says that they are known *to us* as a result of induction from sense-experience. Thus he *seems* to be either a Platonist or an empiricist, according as you choose to remember one set of his utterances or another, and this apparent inconsistency has led to his authority being claimed in their favour by thinkers of the most widely different types. But more careful study will show that the seeming confusion is due to the fact that he tries to combine in one statement his answers to two quite different questions: (1) how we come to reflect on the axioms, (2) what evidence there is for their truth. To the first question he replies, "by induction from experience," and so far he might seem to be a precursor of John Stuart Mill. Successive repetitions of the same sense-perceptions give rise to a single experience, and it is by reflection on experience that we become aware of the most ultimate simple and universal principles. We might illustrate his point by considering how the thought that two and two are four may be brought before a child's mind. We might first take two apples, and two other apples, and set the child to count them. By repeating the process with different apples we may teach the child to dissociate the result of the counting from the particular apples employed, and to advance to the thought, "any two apples and any two other apples make four apples." Then we might substitute pears or cherries for the apples, so as to suggest the thought, "two fruits and two fruits make four fruits." And by similar methods we should in the end evoke the thought, "any two objects whatever and any other two objects whatever make four objects." This exactly illustrates Aristotle's conception of the function of induction, or comparison of instances, in fixing attention

37

on a universal principle of which one had not been conscious before the comparison was made.

Now comes in the point where Aristotle differs wholly from all empiricists, later and earlier. Mill regards the instances produced in the induction as having a double function: they not merely fix the attention on the principle, they also are the evidence of its truth. This gives rise to the greatest difficulty in his whole logical theory. Induction by imperfect enumeration is pronounced to be (as it clearly is) fallacious, yet the principle of the uniformity of Nature which Mill regards as the ultimate premiss of all science, is itself supposed to be proved by this radically fallacious method. Aristotle avoids a similar inconsistency by holding that the sole function of the induction is to fix our attention on a principle which it does not prove. He holds that ultimate principles neither permit of nor require proof. When the induction has done its work in calling attention to the principle, you have to see for yourself that the principle is true. You see that it is true by immediate inspection, just as in sense-perception you have to see that the colour before your eyes is red or blue. This is why Aristotle holds that the knowledge of the principles of science is not itself science (demonstrated knowledge), but what he calls intelligence, and we may call intellectual intuition. Thus his doctrine is sharply distinguished not only from empiricism (the doctrine that universal principles are proved by particular facts), but also from all theories of the Hegelian type which regard the principles and the facts as somehow reciprocally proving each other, and from the doctrine of some eminent modern logicians who hold that "self-evidence" is not required in the ultimate principles of science, as we are only concerned in logic with the question what consequences follow from our initial assumptions, and not with the truth or falsehood of the assumptions themselves.

The result is that Aristotle does little more than repeat the Platonic view of the nature of science. Science consists of deductions from universal principles which sensible experience "suggests," but into which, as they are apprehended by a purely intellectual inspection, no sense-data enter as constituents. The apparent rejection of "transcendental moonshine" has, after all, led to nothing. The only difference between Plato and his scholar lies in the clearness of intellectual vision which Plato shows when he expressly maintains in plain words that the universals of exact science are not "in" our sense-perceptions and therefore to be extracted from them by a process of abstraction, but are "apart from" or "over" them, and form an ideal system of interconnected concepts which the experiences of sense merely "imitate" or make approximation to.

One more point remains to be considered to complete our outline of the Aristotelian theory of knowledge. The sciences have "principles" which are discerned to be true by immediate inspection. But what if one man professes to see the self-evident truth of such an alleged principle, while another is doubtful of its truth, or even denies it? There can be no question of silencing the objector by a demonstration, since no genuine simple principle admits of demonstration. All that can be done—*e.g.* if a man doubts whether things equal to the same thing are equal to one another, or whether the law of contradiction is true—is to examine the consequences of a denial of the axiom and to show that they include some which are false, or which your antagonist at least considers false. In this way, by showing the falsity of consequences which follow from the denial of a given "principle," you indirectly establish its truth. Now reasoning of this kind differs from "science" precisely in the point that you take as your major premiss, not what you regard as true, but the opposite thesis of your antagonist, which you regard as false. Your object is not to prove a true conclusion but to show your opponent that *his* premisses lead to false conclusions. This is "dialectical" reasoning in Aristotle's sense of the word—*i.e.* reasoning not from your own but from some one else's premisses. Hence the chief philosophical importance which Aristotle ascribes to "dialectic" is that it provides a method of defending the undemonstrable axioms against objections. Dialectic of this kind became highly important in the mediaeval Aristotelianism of the schoolmen, with whom it became a regular method, as may be seen *e.g.* in the *Summa* of St. Thomas, to begin their consideration of a doctrine by a preliminary rehearsal of all the arguments they could find or devise against the conclusion they meant to adopt. Thus the first division of any article in the *Summa Theologiae* of Thomas is regularly constituted by arguments based on the premisses of actual or possible antagonists, and is strictly dialectical. (To be quite accurate Aristotle should, of course, have observed that this dialectical method of defending a principle becomes useless in the case of a logical axiom which is presupposed by all deduction. For this reason Aristotle falls into fallacy when he tries to defend the law of contradiction by dialectic. It is true that if the law be denied, then any and every predicate may be indifferently ascribed to any subject. But until the law of contradiction has been admitted, you have no right to regard it as absurd to ascribe all predicates indiscriminately to all subjects. Thus, it is only assumed laws which are *not* ultimate laws of logic that admit of dialectical justification. If a truth is so ultimate that it has either to be recognised by direct inspection or not at all, there can be no arguing at all with one who cannot or will not see it.)

FIRST PHILOSOPHY   III

FIRST
Philosophy is defined by Aristotle as a "science which considers What Is simply in its character of Being, and the properties which it has as such." That there is, or ought to be, such a science is urged on the ground that every "special" science deals only with some restricted department of what is, and thus considers its subject-matter not universally in its character of being, or being real, but as determined by some more special condition. Thus, First Philosophy, the science which attempts to discover the most ultimate reasons of, or grounds for, the character of things in general cannot be identified with any of the "departmental" sciences. The same consideration explains why it is "First Philosophy" which has to disentangle the "principles" of the various sciences, and defend them by dialectic against those who impugn them. It is no part of the duty of a geometer or a physicist to deal with objections to such universal principles of reasoning as the law of contradiction. They may safely assume such principles; if they are attacked, it is not by specifically geometrical or physical considerations that they can be defended. Even the "principles of the special sciences" have not to be examined and defended by the special sciences.

They are the starting-points of the sciences which employ them; these sciences are therefore justified in requiring that they shall be admitted as a condition of geometrical, or physical, or biological demonstrations. If they are called in question, the defence of them is the business of logic.

First Philosophy, then, is the study of "What Is simply as such," the universal principles of structure without which there could be no ordered system of knowable objects. But the word "is" has more than one sense. There are as many modes of being as there are types of predication. "Substances," men, horses, and the like, have their own specific mode of being—they are things; qualities, such as green or sweet, have a different mode of being—they are not things, but "affections" or "attributes" of things. Actions, again, such as building, killing, are neither things nor yet "affections" of things; their mode of being is that they are processes which produce or destroy things. First Philosophy is concerned with the general character of all these modes of being, but it is specially concerned with that mode of being which belongs to *substances*. For this is the most primary of all modes of being. We had to introduce a reference to it in our attempt to say what the mode of being of qualities and actions is, and it would have been the same had our illustrations been drawn from any other "categories." Hence the central and special problem of First Philosophy is to analyse the notion of substance and to show the causes of the existence of substances.

Next, we have to note that the word "substance" itself has two senses. When we spoke of substance as one of the categories we were using it in a secondary sense. We meant by substances "horse," "man," and the rest of the "real kinds" which we find in Nature, and try to reproduce in a scientific classification. In this sense of the word "substances" are a special class of *predicates*, as when we affirm of Plato that he is a man, or of Bucephalus that he is a horse. But in the primary sense a substance means an absolutely individual thing, "*this* man," or "*this* horse." We may therefore define primary substances from the logician's point of view by saying that they can be only subjects of predication, never predicates. Or again, it is peculiar to substances, that while remaining numerically one a substance admits of incompatible determinations, as Socrates, remaining one and the same Socrates, is successively young and old. This is not true of "qualities," "actions," and the rest. The same colour cannot be first white and then black; the same act cannot be first bad and then good. Thus we may say that individual substances are the fixed and permanent factors in the world of mutability, the invariants of existence. Processes go on *in* them, they run the gamut of changes from birth to decay, processes take place *among* them, they act on and are acted on by one another, they fluctuate in their qualities and their magnitude, but so long as a substance exists it remains numerically one and the same throughout all these changes. Their existence is the first and most fundamental condition of the existence of the universe, since they are the bearers of all qualities, the terms of all relations, and the agents and patients in all interaction.

The point to note is that Aristotle begins his investigation into the structure of What Is and the causes by which it is produced by starting from the existence of individual things belonging to the physical order and perceived by the senses. About any such thing we may ask two questions, (1) into what constituent factors can it be logically analysed? (2) and how has it come to exhibit the character which our analysis shows it to have? The answer to these questions will appear from a consideration of two standing antitheses which run through Aristotle's philosophy, the contrast between Matter and Form, and that between Potential and Actual, followed by a recapitulation of his doctrine of the Four Causes, or four senses of the word Cause.

MATTER AND FORM

Consider any completely developed individual thing, whether it is the product of human manufacture, as a copper bowl, or of natural reproduction, as an oak-tree or a horse. We shall see at once that the bowl is like other articles made of the same metal, candlesticks, coal-vases, in being made of the same stuff, and unlike them in having the special shape or structure which renders it fit for being used as a bowl and not for holding a candle or containing coals. So a botanist or a chemist will tell you that the constituent tissues of an oak or horse, or the chemical elements out of which these tissues are built up are of the same kind as those of an ash or an ox, but the oak differs from the ash or the horse from the ox in characteristic structure. We see thus that in any individual thing we can distinguish two components, the stuff of which it consists—which may be identical in kind with the stuff of which things of a very different kind consist—and the structural law of formation or arrangement which is peculiar to the "special" kind of thing under consideration. In the actual individual thing these two are inseparably united; they do not exist side by side, as chemists say the atoms of hydrogen and oxygen do in a drop of water; the law of organisation or structure is manifested in and through the copper, or the various tissues of the living body. Aristotle expresses this by saying that you can distinguish two aspects in an individual, its Matter (*hyle, materia*), and its Form (*eidos, forma*). The individual *is* the matter as organised in accord with a determinate principle of structure, the form. Of these terms, the former, *hyle* (*materia, matter*) means literally timber, and more specifically ship's timbers, and the selection of it to mean what is most exactly rendered by our own word "stuff" may perhaps be due to a reminiscence of an old Pythagorean fancy which looked on the universe as a ship. The word for form is the same as Plato's, and its philosophical uses are closely connected with its mathematical sense, "regular figure," also a Pythagorean technicality which still survives in certain stereotyped phrases in Euclid. Aristotle extends the analysis into Matter and Form by analogy beyond the range of individual substances to everything in which we can distinguish a relatively indeterminate "somewhat" and a law or type of order and arrangement giving it determination. Thus if we consider the relatively fixed or "formed" character of a man in adult life, we may look upon this character as produced out of the "raw material" of tendencies and dispositions, which have received a specific development along definite lines, according to the kind of training to which the mind has been subjected in the "formative" period of its growth. We may therefore speak of native disposition as the matter or stuff of which character is made, and the practical problem of education is to devise a system of training which shall impress on this matter precisely the form required if the grown man is to be a good citizen of a good state. Since a man's character itself is not a substance but a complex of habits or fixed ways of reacting upon suggestions coming from the world around him, this is a good instance of the extension of the antithesis of Matter and Form beyond the category of substance. We see then that Matter in the Aristotelian sense must not be confounded with body; the relatively undetermined factor which receives completer determination by the structural law or Form is Matter, whether it is corporeal or not. This comes out with particular clearness in the metaphysical interpretation put on

45

the logical process of definition by genus and difference. When I define any real kind by specifying a higher and wider class of which it is a sub-kind, and adding the peculiar characteristics which distinguish the sub-kind under consideration from the other sub-kinds of the same genus, the genus may be said to stand to the "differences" as Matter, the relatively indeterminate, to the Form which gives it its structure.

We further observe that Matter and Form are strictly correlative. The matter is called so relatively to the form which gives it further determination. When the words are used in their strictest sense, with reference to an individual thing, the Form is taken to mean the *last* determination by which the thing acquires its complete character, and the Matter is that which has yet to receive this last determination. Thus in the case of a copper globe, the spherical figure is said to be its Form, the copper its material. In the case of the human body, the Matter is the various tissues, muscles, bones, skin, etc. But each of these things which are counted as belonging to the Matter of the globe or the human body has, according to Aristotle, a development behind it. Copper is not an "element" but a specific combination of "elements," and the same thing is even more true of the highly elaborate tissues of the living body. Thus what is Matter relatively to the globe or living body is Matter already determined by Form if we consider it relatively to its own constituents. The so-called "elements" of Empedocles, earth, water, air, fire, are the matter of all chemical compounds, the Form of each compound being its specific law of composition; the immediate or "proximate" Matter of the tissues of the animal body is, according to Aristotle's biology, the "superfluous" blood of the female parent, out of which the various tissues in the offspring are developed, and the Matter of this blood is in turn the various substances which are taken into the body of the parent as food and converted by assimilation into blood. Their Matter, once more, is the earth, air, fire, and water of which they are composed. Thus at every stage of a process of manufacture or growth a fresh Form is superinduced on, or developed within, a Matter which is already itself a combination of Matter and Form relatively to the process by which it has itself been originated. Fully thought out, such a view would lead to the conclusion that in the end the simple ultimate matter of all individual things is one and the same throughout the universe, and has absolutely no definite structure at all. The introduction of Form or determinate structure of any kind would then have to be thought of as coming from an outside source, since structureless Matter cannot be supposed to give itself all sorts of specific determinations, as has been demonstrated in our own times by the collapse of the "Synthetic Philosophy." Aristotle avoids the difficulty by holding that "pure Matter" is a creation of our thought. In actual fact the crudest form in which matter is found is that of the "elements." Since the transmutability of the "elements" is an indispensable tenet in Aristotle's Physics, we cannot avoid regarding earth, water, fire, air, as themselves determinations by specific Form of a still simpler Matter, though this "prime Matter" "all alone, before a rag of Form is on," is never to be found existing in its simplicity.*

THE POTENTIAL AND THE ACTUAL

So far we have been looking at the analysis of the individual thing, as the current jargon puts it, statically; we have

---

* *Hudibras*, Pt. I, Canto I, 560.
  "He had First Matter seen undressed;
  He took her naked all alone,
  Before one rag of Form was on."

arrived at the antithesis of Matter and Form by contrasting an unfinished condition of anything with its finished condition. But we may study the same contrast dynamically, with special reference to the process of making or growth by which the relatively undetermined or unfinished becomes determined or finished. The contrast of Matter with Form then passes into the contrast between Potentiality and Actuality. What this antithesis means we can best see from the case of the growth of a living organism. Consider the embryos of two animals, or the seeds of two plants. Even a botanist or a physiologist may be unable to pronounce with certainty on the species to which the germ submitted to him belongs, and chemical analysis may be equally at a loss. Even at a later stage of development, the embryo of one vertebrate animal may be indistinguishable from that of another. Yet it is certain that one of two originally indistinguishable germs will grow into an oak and the other into an elm, or one into a chimpanzee and the other into a man. However indistinguishable, they therefore may be said to have different latent tendencies or possibilities of development within them. Hence we may say of a given germ, "though this is not yet actually an oak, it is potentially an oak," meaning not merely that, if uninterfered with, it will in time be an oak, but also that by no interference can it be made to grow into an elm or a beech. So we may look upon all processes of production or development as processes by which what at first possessed only the tendency to grow along certain lines or to be worked up into a certain form, has become actually endowed with the character to which it possessed the tendency. The acorn becomes in process of time an actual oak, the baby an actual man, the copper is made into an actual vase, right education brings out into active exercise the special capacities of the learner. Hence the distinction between Matter and Form may also be expressed by saying that the Matter is the persistent underlying *substratum* in which the development of the Form takes place, or that the individual when finally determined by the Form is the Actuality of which the undeveloped Matter was the Potentiality. The process of conception, birth, and growth to maturity in Nature, or of the production of a finished article by the "arts" whose business it is to "imitate" Nature, may be said to be one of continuous advance towards the actual embodiment of a Form, or law of organisation, in a Matter having the latent potentiality of developing along those special lines. When Aristotle is speaking most strictly he distinguishes the process by which a Form is realised, which he calls Energeia, from the manifestation of the realised Form, calling the latter Entelechy (literally "finished" or "completed" condition). Often, however, he uses the word Energeia more loosely for the actual manifestation of the Form itself, and in this he is followed by the scholastic writers, who render Energeia by *actus* or *actus purus*.

One presupposition of this process must be specially noted. It is not an unending process of development of unrealised capacities, but always has an End in the perfectly simple sense of a last stage. We see this best in the case of growth. The acorn grows into the sapling and the sapling into the oak, but there is nothing related to the oak as the oak is to the sapling. The oak does not grow into something else. The process of development from potential to actual in this special case comes to an end with the emergence of the mature oak. In the organic world the end or last state is recognised by the fact that the organism can now exercise the power of reproducing its like. This tendency of organic process to culminate in a last stage of complete maturity is the key to the treatment of the problem of the "true end" of life in Aristotle's *Ethics*.

THE FOUR CAUSES

The conception of the world involved in these antitheses of Form and Matter, Potential and Actual, finds its fullest expression in Aristotle's doctrine of the Four Causes or conditions of the production of things. This doctrine is looked on by Aristotle as the final solution of the problem which had always been the central one for Greek philosophy, What are the causes of the world-order? All the previous philosophies he regards as inadequate attempts to formulate the answer to this question which is only given completely by his own system. Hence the doctrine requires to be stated with some fullness. We may best approach it by starting from the literal meaning of the Greek terms *aitia, aition*, which Aristotle uses to convey the notion of cause. *Aition* is properly an adjective used substantivally, and means "that on which the legal responsibility for a given state of affairs can be laid." Similarly *aitia*, the substantive, means the "credit" for good or bad, the legal "responsibility," for an act. Now when we ask, "what is responsible for the fact that such and such a state of things now exists?" there are four partial answers which may be given, and each of these corresponds to one of the "causes." A complete answer requires the enumeration of them all. We may mention (1) the *matter* or *material cause* of the thing, (2) the law according to which it has grown or developed, the *form* or *formal* cause, (3) the agent with whose initial impulse the development began—the "starting-point of the process," or, as the later Aristotelians call it, the *efficient* cause, (4) the completed result of the whole process, which is present in the case of human manufacture as a preconceived idea determining the maker's whole method of handling his material, and in organic development in Nature as implied in and determining the successive stages of growth—the *end* or *final*

cause. If any one of these had been different, the resultant
state of things would also have been different. Hence all four
must be specified in completely accounting for it. Obvious
illustrations can be given from artificial products of human
skill, but it seems clear that it was rather reflection on the
biological process of reproduction and growth which
originally suggested the analysis. Suppose we ask what was
requisite in order that there should be now an oak on a given
spot. There must have been (1) a germ from which the oak
has grown, and this germ must have had the latent tendencies
towards development which are characteristic of oaks. This
is the material cause of the oak. (2) This germ must have
followed a definite law of growth; it must have had a
tendency to grow in the way characteristic of oaks and to
develop the structure of an oak, not that of a plane or an ash.
This is form or formal cause. (3) Also the germ of the oak
did not come from nowhere; it grew on a parent oak. The
parent oak and its acorn-bearing activity thus constitute the
efficient cause of the present oak. (4) And there must be a
final stage to which the whole process of growth is relative,
in which the germ or sapling is no longer becoming but *is* an
adult oak bearing fresh acorns. This is the *end* of the process.
One would not be going far wrong in saying that Aristotle's
biological cast of thought leads him to conceive of this "end"
in the case of reproduction as a sub-conscious purpose, just
as the workman's thought of the result to be attained by his
action forms a conscious directing purpose in the case of
manufacture. Both in Nature and in "art" the "form," the
"efficient cause," and the "end" tend to coalesce. Thus in
Nature "a man begets a man," organic beings give birth to
other organic beings of the same *kind*, or, in the technical
language of the Aristotelian theory of Causation, the
efficient cause produces, as the "end" of its action, a second
being having the same "form" as itself, though realised in

51

different "matter," and numerically distinct from itself. Thus the efficient cause (*i.e.* the parent) is a "form" realised in matter, and the "end" is the same "form" realised in other matter. So in "products of art" the true "source of the process" is the "form" the realisation of which is the "end" or final cause, only with this difference, that as efficient cause the "form" exists not in the material but by way of "idea" or "representation" in the mind of the craftsman. A house does not produce another house, but the house as existing in "idea" in the builder's mind sets him at work building, and so produces a corresponding house in brick or stone. Thus the ultimate opposition is between the "cause as matter," a passive and inert substratum of change and development and the "formal" cause which, in the sense just explained, is one with both the "efficient" or starting-point, and the "end" or goal of development. It will, of course, be seen that individual bearers of "forms" are indispensable in the theory; hence the notion of *activity* is essential to the causal relation. It is a relation between things, not between events. Aristotle has no sense of the word cause corresponding to Mill's conception of a cause as an event which is the uniform precursor of another event.

Two more remarks may be made in this connection. (1) The prominence of the notion of "end" gives Aristotle's philosophy a thorough-going "teleological" character. God and Nature, he tells us, do nothing aimlessly. We should probably be mistaken if we took this to mean that "God and Nature" act everywhere with conscious design. The meaning is rather that every natural process has a last stage in which the "form" which was to begin with present in the agent or "source of change" is fully realised in the matter in which the agent has set up the process of change. The normal thing is *e.g.* for animals to reproduce "their kind"; if the reproduction is imperfect or distorted, as in monstrous births, this is an exception due to the occasional presence in "matter" of imperfections which hinder the course of development, and must be regarded as "contrary to the normal course of Nature." So hybrid reproduction is exceptional and "against Nature," and this is shown by the sterility of hybrids, a sort of lesser monstrosity. Even females, being "arrested developments," are a sort of still minor deviation from principle. (2) It may just be mentioned that Aristotle has a classification of efficient causes under the three heads of Nature, Intelligence (or Man), and Chance. The difference between Nature and Man or Intelligence as efficient causes has already been illustrated. It is that in causation by Nature, such as sexual reproduction, or the assimilation of nutriment, or the conversion of one element into another in which Aristotle believed, the form which is superinduced on the matter by the agent already exists in the agent itself as *its* form. The oak springs from a parent oak, the conversion of nutriment into organic tissue is due to the agency of already existing organic tissue. In the case of human intelligence or art, the "form" to be superinduced exists in the agent not as *his* characteristic form, but by way of representation, as a contemplated design. The man who builds a house is not himself a house; the form characteristic of a house is very different from that characteristic of a man, but it is present in contemplation to the builder before it is embodied in the actual house. A word may be added about the third sort of efficient causality, causation by chance. This is confined to cases which are exceptions from the general course of Nature, remarkable coincidences. It is what we may call "simulated purposiveness." When something in human affairs happens in a way which subserves the achievement of a result but was not really brought about by any intention to secure the result, we speak of it as a remarkable coincidence. Thus it would be a coincidence if a man should be held to ransom by brigands and his best friend should, without knowing anything of the matter, turn up on the spot with the means of ransoming him. The events could not have happened more opportunely if they had been planned, and yet they were not planned but merely fell out so; and since such a combination of circumstances simulating design is unusual, it is not proper to say that the events happened "in the course of Nature." We therefore say it happened by chance. This doctrine of chance has its significance for mediaeval Ethics. In an age when the Protestant super-stition that worldly success is proof of nearness to God had not yet been invented, the want of correspondence between men's "deserts" and their prosperity was accounted for by the view that the distribution of worldly goods is, as a rule, the work of Fortune or Chance in the Aristotelian sense; that is, it is due to special coincidences which may look like deliberate design but are not really so. (See the elaborate exposition of this in Dante, *Inferno*, vii. 67–97.)

MOTION

We have seen that causation, natural or artificial, requires the production in a certain "matter" of a certain "form" under the influence of a certain "agent." What is the character of the process set up by the agent in the matter and culminating in the appearance of the form? Aristotle answers that it is Motion (*kinesis*). The effect of the agent on the matter is to set up in it a motion which ends in its assuming a definite form. The important point to be noted here is that Aristotle regards this motion as falling wholly within the matter which is to assume the form. It is not necessary that the agent should itself be in motion, but only that it should induce motion in something else. Thus in all

54

cases of intentional action the ultimate efficient cause is the "idea of the result to be attained," but this idea does not move about. By its presence to the mind it sets something else (the members of the body) moving. This conception of an efficient cause which, not moving itself, by its mere presence induces movement in that to which it is present, is of the highest importance in Aristotle's theology. Of course it follows that since the motion by which the transition from potentiality to actuality is achieved falls wholly within the matter acted upon, Aristotle is not troubled with any of the questions as to the way in which motion can be transferred from one body to another which were so much agitated in the early days of the modern mechanical interpretation of natural processes. Aristotle's way of conceiving Nature is thoroughly non-mechanical, and approximates to what would now be called the ascription of vital or quasi-vital characteristics to the inorganic. As, in the causality of "art" the mere presence of the "form" to be embodied in a given material to the mind of the craftsman brings about and directs the process of manufacture, so in some analogous fashion the presence of an efficient cause in Nature to that on which it works is thought of as itself constituting the "efficiency" of the cause. As Lotze phrases it, things "take note of" one another's compresence in the universe, or we might say the efficient cause and that on which it exercises its efficiency are *en rapport*. "Matter" is sensitive to the presence of the "efficient cause," and in response to this sensitivity, puts forth successive determinations, expands its latent tendencies on definite lines.

The name "motion" has a wider sense for Aristotle than it has for ourselves. He includes under the one common name all the processes by which things come to be what they are or cease to be what they have been. Thus he distinguishes the following varieties of "motion": *generation* (the coming of an individual thing into being), with its opposite *decay* or *corruption* (the passing of a thing out of being), *alteration* (change of *quality* in a thing), *augmentation* and *diminution* (change in the *magnitude* of a thing), *motion through space* (of which latter he recognises two sub-species, rectilinear *transference* and *rotation* in a circular orbit about an axis). It is this last variety, motion through space, which is the most fundamental of all, since its occurrence is involved in that of any of the other types of process mentioned, though Aristotle does not hold the thorough-going mechanical view that the other processes are only apparent, and that, as we might put it, qualitative change is a mere disguise which mechanical motion wears for our senses.

THE ETERNITY OF MOTION

Certain very important consequences follow from the conception of efficient causation which we have been describing. Aristotle has no sympathy with the "evolutionist" views which had been favoured by some of his predecessors. According to his theory of organic generation, "it takes a man to beget a man"; where there is a baby, there must have been a father. Biological kinds representing real clefts in Nature, the process of the production of a young generation by an already adult generation must be thought of as without beginning and without end. There can be no natural "evolution" of animals of one species from individuals of a different kind. Nor does it occur to Aristotle to take into account the possibility of "Creationism," the sudden coming into being of a fully fledged first generation at a stroke. This possibility is excluded by the doctrine that the "matter" of a thing must exist beforehand as an indispensable condition of the production of that thing. Every baby, as we said, must have had a father, but that father must also have been a baby before he was a full-grown man. Hence the perpetuation of unchanging species must be without beginning and without end. And it is implied that all the various processes, within and without the organism, apart from which its life could not be kept up, must be equally without beginning and without end. The "cosmos," or orderly world of natural processes, is strictly "eternal"; "motion" is everlasting and continuous, or unbroken. Even the great Christian theologians who built upon Aristotle could not absolutely break with him on this point. St. Thomas, though obliged to admit that the world was actually created a few thousand years before his own time, maintains that this can only be known to be true from revelation, philosophically it is equally tenable that the world should have been "created from all eternity." And it is the general doctrine of scholasticism that the expression "creation" only denotes the absolute dependence of the world on God for its being. When we say "God created the world out of nothing," we mean that He did not make it out of pre-existing matter, that it depends for its being on Him only; the expression is purely negative in its import.

GOD

With the doctrine of the eternity of the world and the processes which make up its life we come close to the culminating theory of Aristotelian First Philosophy, its doctrine of God, as the eternal, unchanging source of all change, movement, and process. All motion is a process within matter by which the forms latent in it are brought into actual manifestation. And the process only takes place in the presence of an adequate efficient cause or source of motion. Hence the eternity of natural processes involves the existence of one or more eternal sources of motion. For, if we do not admit the existence of an unoriginated and ever-present source or sources of motion, our only alternative is to hold that the world-process is due to a series of sources of motion existing successively. But such a view would leave the unity and unbroken continuity of the world-process unaccounted for. It would give us a succession of processes, temporally contiguous, not one unbroken process. Hence we argue from the continuity of motion to its dependence on a source or sources which are permanent and present throughout the whole everlasting world-process. And when we come to the question whether there is only one such ultimate source of movement for the whole universe, or several, Aristotle's answer is that the supreme "Unmoved Mover" is one. One is enough for the purpose, and the law of parsimony forbids us to assume the superfluous. This then is the Aristotelian conception of God and God's relation to the world. God is the one supreme unchanging being to whose presence the world responds with the whole process of cosmic development, the ultimate educer of the series of "forms" latent in the "matter" of the world into actual manifestation. Standing, as He does, outside the whole process which by His mere presence He initiates in Nature, He is not Himself a composite of "form" and "matter," as the products of development are. He is a pure individual "form" or "actuality," with no history of gradual development behind it. Thus He is a purely immaterial being, indispensable to the world's existence, but transcending it and standing outside it. *How* His presence inspires the world to move Aristotle tries to explain by the metaphor of appetition. Just as the good I desire and conceive, without itself "moving" "moves" my appetition, so God moves the universe by being its good. This directly brings about a uniform unbroken rotation of the whole universe round its axis (in fact, the alternation of day and night). And since this rotation is communicated from the outermost "sphere" of heaven to all the lesser "spheres" between it and the immovable centre, the effects of God's presence are felt universally. At the same time, we must note that though God is the supreme Mover of the Universe, He is not regarded by Aristotle as its Creator, even in the sense in which creation can be reconciled with the eternity of the world. For the effect of God's presence is simply to lead to the development of "form" in an already existing "matter." Without God there could be no "form" or order in things, not even as much aₓ is implied in the differentiation of matter into the four "elements," yet "primary matter" is no less than God a precondition of all that happens.

It is characteristic of Aristotle that his God is as far from discharging the functions of a Providence as He is from being a Creator. His "activity" is not, as Plato had made it, that of the great "Shepherd of the sheep." As far as the world is concerned, God's only function is to be there to move its appetition. For the rest, the unbroken activity of His life is directed wholly inward. Aristotle expressly calls it an "activity of immobility." More precisely, he tells us, it is activity of thought, exercised unbrokenly and everlastingly upon the only object adequate to exercise God's contemplation, Himself. His life is one of everlasting *self*-contemplation or "thinking of thought itself." Like all unimpeded exercise of activity, it is attended by pleasure, and as the activity is continuous, so the pleasure of it is continuous too. At our best, when we give ourselves up to the pure contemplative activity of scientific thought or aesthetic appreciation, we enter for a while into this divine life and share the happiness of God. But that is a theme for our chapter on the *Ethics*.

It is a far cry from this conception of a God untroubled by care for a world to which He is only related as the object of its aspiration to the God who cares even for the fall of the sparrow and of whom it is written, *Sic Deus dilexit mundum*, but it was the standing task of the philosophical theologians of the Middle Ages to fuse the two conceptions. Plato's God, who, if not quite the Creator, is the "Father and Fashioner" of us all, and keeps providential watch over the world He has fashioned, would have lent Himself better to their purposes, but Plato was held by the mediaeval church to have denied the resurrection of the body.* The combination of Aristotle's Theism with the Theism of early Christianity was effected by exquisitely subtle logical devices, but even in St. Thomas one cannot help seeing the seams.

Nor can one help seeing in Aristotle's own doctrine the usual want of coherence between an initial anti-Platonic bias and a final reversion to the very Platonic positions Aristotle is fond of impugning. We are told at the outset that the Platonic "separate forms" are empty names, and that the real individual thing is always a composite of matter and a form which only exists "in matter." We find in the end that the source of the whole process by which "matter" becomes imbued with "form" is a being which is "pure" form and stands outside the whole development which its presence sets up. And the issue of Aristotle's warning against "poetic metaphors" is the doctrine that God moves the world by being "the object of the world's desire."

* Because in the *Phaedo* he makes Socrates speak of the "saints" as living "wholly freed from the body."

PHYSICS

IV

no part of Aristotle's system which has been more carefully
thought out than his Physics; at the same time it is almost
wholly on account of his physical doctrines that his long
ascendancy over thought is so much to be regretted.
Aristotle's qualifications as a man of science have been much
overrated. In one department, that of descriptive natural
history, he shows himself a master of minute and careful
observation who could obtain unqualified praise from so
great a naturalist as Darwin. But in Astronomy and Physics
proper his inferiority in mathematical thinking and his dislike for mechanical ways of explaining facts put him at a
great disadvantage, as compared with Plato and Plato's
Pythagorean friends. Thus his authority was for centuries
one of the chief influences which prevented the development
of Astronomy on right lines. Plato had himself taught the
mobility of the earth and denied correctly that the earth is at
the centre of the universe, and the "Copernican" hypothesis
in Astronomy probably originated in the Academy. Aristotle, however, insists on the central position of the earth,
and violently attacks Plato for believing in its motion. It is
equally serious that he insists on treating the so-called "four

elements" as ultimately unanalysable forms of matter, though Plato had not only observed that so far from being the A B C (*stoicheia* or *elementa*, literally, letters of the alphabet) of Nature they do not deserve to be called even "syllables," but had also definitely put forward the view that it is the geometrical structure of the "corpuscles" of body upon which sensible qualities depend.* It is on this doctrine, of course, that all mathematical physics rests. Aristotle reverts to the older theory that the differences between one "element" and another are qualitative differences of a sensible kind. Even in the biological sciences Aristotle shows an unfortunate proneness to disregard established fact when it conflicts with the theories for which he has a personal liking. Thus, though the importance of the brain as the central organ of the sensori-motor system had been discovered in the late sixth or early fifth century by the physician Alcmaeon of Crotona, and taught by the great Hippocrates in the fifth and by Plato in the fourth century, Aristotle's prejudices in favour of the doctrines of a different school of biologists led him to revert to the view that it is the heart which is the centre of what we now call the "nervous system." It is mainly on account of these reactionary scientific views that he was attacked in the early seventeenth century by writers like our own Francis Bacon, who found in veneration for Aristotle one of the chief hindrances to the free development of natural science. The same complaints had been made long before by critics belonging to the Platonic Academy. It is a Platonist of the time of Marcus Aurelius who sums up a vigorous attack on the Aristotelian astronomy by the remark that Aristotle never understood

---

* Plato does not even claim to be the author of the doctrine, which he ascribes to the Pythagoreans of the age of Socrates.

that the true task of the physicist is not to prescribe laws to Nature, but to learn from observation of the facts what the laws followed by Nature are.

In determining the scope of Physics, we have to begin by considering what is the special characteristic of things produced by Nature as contrasted with those produced by "art." The obvious distinction, intimated by the very etymology of the word "Nature" (*physis*, connected with *phyesthai*, to grow, to be born, as *natura* is with *nasci*), is that "what is by Nature" is born and grows, whereas what is as a result of artifice is *made*. The "natural" may thus be said to consist of living bodies and of their constituent parts. Hence inorganic matter also is included in "Nature," on the ground that living tissue can be analysed back into compounds of the "elements." Now things which are alive and grow are distinguished from things which are made by "a source of motion and quiescence within themselves"; all of them exhibit motions, changes of quality, processes of growth and decline which are initiated from within. Hence Nature may be defined as the totality of things which have a source of motion internal to themselves and of the constituent parts of such things. Nature then comprises all beings capable of spontaneous change. Whatever either does not change at all, or only changes in consequence of external influences, is excluded from Nature.*

Thus the fundamental fact everywhere present in Nature is "change," "process," "motion." Since motion in the literal sense of change of position is involved as a condition of every such process, and such motion requires space through which to move and time to move in, the doctrine

---

* Even the "elements," according to Aristotle, exhibit "spontaneity." Earth *e.g.* *spontaneously* falls *downwards*, fire and air rise *upwards*.

of space and time will also form part of Physics. Hence a great part of Aristotle's special lectures on Physics is occupied with discussion of the nature of space and time, and of the continuity which we must ascribe to them if the "continuous motion" on which the unbroken life of the universe depends is to be real. Aristotle knows nothing of the modern questions whether space and time are "real" or only "phenomenal," whether they are "objective" or "subjective." Just as he simply assumes that bodies are things that really exist, whether we happen to perceive them or not, so he assumes that the space and time in which they move are real features of a world that does not depend for its existence on our perceiving it.

His treatment of space is singularly *naïf*. He conceives it as a sort of vessel, into which you can pour different liquids. Just as the same pot may hold first wine and then water, so, if you can say, "there was water here, but now there is air here," this implies the existence of a receptacle which once held the water, but now holds the air. Hence a jug or pot may be called a "place that can be carried about," and space or place may be called "an immovable vessel." Hence the "place" of a thing may be defined as the boundary, or inner surface, of the body which immediately surrounds the thing. It follows from this that there can be no empty space. In the last resort, "absolute space" is the actual surface of the outermost "heaven" which contains everything else in itself but is not contained in any remoter body. Thus all things whatever are "in" this "heaven." But it is not itself "in" anything else. In accord with the standing Greek identification of determinate character with limitation, Aristotle holds that this outermost heaven must be at a limited distance from us. Actual space is thus finite in the sense that the volume of the universe could be expressed as a finite number of cubic miles or yards, though, since it must be "continuous," it is infinitely divisible. However often you subdivide a length, an area, or a volume, you will always be dividing it into lesser lengths, etc., which can once more be divided. You will never by division come to "points," *i.e.* mere positions without magnitude of divisibility.

The treatment of time is more thoughtful. Time is inseparably connected with movement or change. We only perceive that time has elapsed when we perceive that change has occurred. But time is not the same as change. For change is of different and incommensurate kinds, change of place, change of colour, etc.; but to take up time is common to all these forms of process. And time is not the same as motion. For there are different rates of speed, but the very fact that we can compare these different velocities implies that there are not different velocities of *time*. Time then is that in terms of which we *measure* motion, "the number of motion in respect of before and after," *i.e.* it is that by which we estimate the *duration* of processes. Thus *e.g.* when we speak of *two* minutes, *two* days, *two* months as required for a certain process to be completed, we are counting something. This something is time. It does not seem to occur to Aristotle that this definition implies that there are indivisible bits of time, though he quite correctly states the incompatible proposition that time is "made up of successive *nows*," *i.e.* moments which have no duration at all, and can no more be counted than the points on a straight line. He recognises of course that the "continuity" of motion implies that of time as well as of space. Since, however, "continuity" in his language means the same thing as indefinite divisibility, it ought not to be possible for him to regard time as "made up of *nows*"; time, like linear extension, ought for him to be a "length of" something.

THE CONTINUOUS MOTION AND THE "SPHERES"

The continuous world-process depends upon a continuous movement set up in the universe as a whole by the presence of an everlasting and unchangeable "First Mover," God. From the self-sameness of God, it follows that this most universal of movements must be absolutely uniform. Of what precise kind can such a movement be? As the source of the movement is one, and the object moved is also one—viz. the compass of the "heaven," the movement of the *primum mobile* or "first moved"—the object immediately stimulated to motion by God's presence to it, must be mechanically simple. Now Aristotle, mistakenly, held that there are two forms of movement which are simple and unanalysable, motion of translation along a straight line, and motion of rotation round an axis. He is at pains to argue that rectilinear motion, which we easily discover to be that characteristic of bodies near the earth's surface when left to themselves, cannot be the kind of movement which belongs to the "heaven" as a whole. For continuous rectilinear movement in the same direction could not go on for ever on his assumption that there is no space outside the "heaven," which is itself at a finite distance from us. And motion to and fro would not be unbroken, since Aristotle argues that every time a moving body reached the end of its path, and the sense of its movement was reversed, it would be for two consecutive moments in the same place, and therefore at rest. Reversal of sense would imply a discontinuity. Hence he decides that the primary unbroken movement must be the rotation of the "first moved"—that is, the heaven containing the fixed stars—round its axis. This is the only movement which could go on for ever at a uniform rate and

in the same sense. Starting with the conviction that the earth
is at rest in the centre of the universe, he inevitably accounts
for the alternation of day and night as the effect of such a
revolution of the whole universe round an axis passing
through the centre of the earth. The universe is thus thought
of as bounded by a spherical surface, on the concave side of
which are the fixed stars, which are therefore one and all at
the same distance from us. This sphere, under the immediate
influence of God, revolves on its axis once in twenty-four
hours, and this period of revolution is absolutely uniform.
Next the apparently irregular paths of the "planets" known
to Aristotle (*i.e.* the moon, Mercury, Venus, the sun, Mars,
Jupiter, Saturn) are resolved into combinations of similar
uniform rotations, each planet having as many "spheres"
assigned to it as are requisite for the analysis of its apparent
path into perfectly circular elementary motions. Altogether
Aristotle holds that fifty-four such rotating spheres are
required over and above the "first moved" itself, whose
rotation is, of course, communicated to all the lesser
"spheres" included within it. As in the case of the "first
moved," the uniform unceasing rotation of each "sphere" is
explained by the influence on it of an unchanging immaterial
"form," which is to its own "sphere" what God is to the
universe as a whole. In the Aristotelianism of the mediaeval
Church these pure forms or intelligences which originate the
movements of the various planetary spheres are naturally
identified with angels. It is *e.g.* to the angelic intelligences
that "move" the heaven of Venus, which comes third in
order counting outward from the earth, that Dante addresses
his famous Canzone, *Voi ch' intendendo il terzo ciel movete*.
The mediaeval astronomy, however, differs in two important respects from that of Aristotle himself. (1) The number
of "spheres" is different. Increasing knowledge of the com-

plexity of the paths of the planets showed that if their paths are to be analysed into combinations of circular motions, fifty-four such rotations must be an altogether inadequate number. Aristotle's method of analysis of the heavenly movements was therefore combined with either or both of two others originated by pure astronomers who sat loose to metaphysics. One of these methods was to account for a planet's path by the introduction of *epicycles*. The planet was thought of not as fixed at a given point on its principal sphere, but as situated on the circumference of a lesser sphere which has its centre at a fixed point of the principal sphere and rotates around an axis passing through this centre. If need were, this type of hypothesis could be further complicated by imagining any number of such epicycles within epicycles. The other method was the employment of "eccentrics," *i.e.* circular movements which are described not about the common centre of the earth and the universe, but about some point in its neighbourhood. By combinations of epicycles and eccentrics the mediaeval astronomers contrived to reduce the number of *principal* spheres to *one* for each planet, the arrangement we find in Dante. (2) Also real or supposed astronomical perturbations unknown to Aristotle led some mediaeval theorists to follow the scheme devised by Alphonso the Wise of Castile, in which further spheres are inserted between that of Saturn, the outermost planet, and the "first moved." In Dante, we have, excluding the "empyrean" or immovable heaven where God and the blessed are, nine "spheres," one for each of the planets, one for the fixed stars, and one for the "first moved," which is now distinguished from the heaven of the stars. In Milton, who adopts the "Alphonsine" scheme, we have further a sphere called the "second movable" or "crystalline" introduced between the heaven of the fixed stars and the "first moved," to account for the imaginary phenomenon of "trepidation."* In reading Dante, Shakespeare, and Milton, we have always to remember that none of these reproduces the Aristotelian doctrine of the "spheres" accurately; their astronomy is an amalgam of Aristotle, Ptolemy, and Hipparchus.

So far, the doctrine of the fifty-five "spheres" might be no more than a legitimate mathematical fiction, a convenient device for analysing the complicated apparent movements of the heavenly bodies into circular components. This was originally the part played by "spheres" in ancient astronomical theory, and it is worth while to be quite clear about the fact, as there is a mistaken impression widely current to-day that Aristotle's astronomy is typical of Greek views in general. The truth is that it is peculiar to himself. The origin of the theory was Academic. Plato proposed to the Academy as a subject of inquiry, to devise such a mathematical analysis of astronomical motions as will best "save the appearances," *i.e.* will most simply account for the apparent paths of the planets. The analysis of these paths into resultants of several rotations was offered as a solution by the astronomer Eudoxus of Cnidus. So far, the "spheres," then, were a mere kinematical hypothesis. What Aristotle did, and it is perhaps the most retrograde step ever taken in the history of a science, was to convert the mathematical hypothesis into physical fact. The "spheres" become with him real bodies, and as none of the bodies we are familiar with exhibit any tendency to rotate in circles when left to themselves, Aristotle was forced to introduce into Physics the disastrous theory, which it was a great part of Galileo's life-work to

---

* *Paradise Lost*, iii. 481.

> "They pass the planets seven, and pass the fixed,
> And that crystalline sphere whose balance weighs
> The trepidation talked, and that first moved."

69

destroy, that the stuff of which the spheres are made is a "fifth body," different from the "elements" of which the bodies among which we live are made. Hence he makes an absolute distinction between two kinds of matter, "celestial matter," the "fifth body," and "terrestrial" or "elementary" matter. The fundamental difference is that "terrestrial" or "elementary" matter, left to itself, follows a rectilinear path, "celestial" matter rotates, but it is further inferred from the supposed absolute uniformity of the celestial movements that "celestial matter" is simple, uncompounded, incapable of change, and consequently that no new state of things can ever arise in the heavens. The spheres and planets have always been and will always be exactly as they are at the present moment. Mutability is confined to the region of "terrestrial" or "elementary" matter, which only extends as far as the orbit of the moon, the "lowest of the celestial bodies," because it is only "terrestrial" things which are, as we should say, chemical compounds. This is the doctrine which Galileo has in mind when he dwells on such newly-discovered astronomical facts as the existence of sun-spots and variable stars, and the signs of irregularity presented by the moon's surface.* The distinction is peculiar to Aristotle. No one before him had ever thought of supposing the heavenly bodies to be made of any materials other than those of which "bodies terrestrial" are made. In the Academic attack on Aristotle's science of which we have already spoken the two points singled out for reprobation are (1) his rejection of the principle that all moving bodies, left to themselves, follow a rectilinear path, and (2) his denial that the heavenly bodies are made of the same "elements" as everything else. (It may just be mentioned in passing that

* For a mediaeval "Aristotelian" explanation of the "face in the moon," see Dante *Paradiso*, ii. 46–105.

our word *quintessence* gets its sense from the supposed special "nobility" of the incorruptible "fifth body.")

TERRESTRIAL BODIES

As we have seen already, Aristotle was out of sympathy with the tendency to regard the sensible differences between bodies as consequences of more ultimate differences in the geometrical structure of their particles. Hence his whole attitude towards the problems of that branch of natural science which *we* call physics is quite unlike any view to which we are accustomed. He reverts from the mathematical lines of thought current in Plato's Academy to the type of view more natural to the "plain man," and, like the earliest sixth-century men of science, regards the *qualitative* differences which our senses apprehend as fundamental. Among these, particular stress is laid on the difference in sensible temperature (the hot—the cold), in saturation (the dry—the moist), and in density (the dense—the rare). If we consider the first two of these oppositions, we can make four binary combinations of the elementary "opposite" characters, viz. hot and dry, hot and moist, cold and moist, cold and dry. These combinations are regarded as corresponding respectively to the sensible characteristics of the four bodies which Empedocles, the father of Greek chemistry, had treated as the ultimate components of everything. Fire is hot and dry, air hot and moist, water moist and cold, earth cold and dry. This reflection shows us why Aristotle held that the most rudimentary form in which "matter" ever actually exists is that of one of these "elements." Each of them has *one* quality in common with another, and it is in virtue of this that a portion of one element can be assimilated by and transmuted into another, a process which seems to the untutored eye to be constantly recurring in Nature. We also observe that the order in which the "elements" appear, when so arranged as to form a series in which each term has one quality in common with each of its neighbours, is that of their increasing density. This would help to make the conception of their transmutability all the more natural, as it suggests that the process may be effected by steady condensation. We must remember carefully that for Aristotle, who denies the possibility of a vacuum, as for the mediaeval alchemists, condensation does not mean a mere diminution of the distances between corpuscles which remain unchanged in character, but is a process of real qualitative change in the body which undergoes it. Incidentally we may remark that *all* changes of quality are regarded by Aristotle as stages in a continuous "movement" from one extreme of a scale to another. For example, colours, with him as with Goethe, form a series of which the "opposites" white and black are the end-points. Every other colour is a combination of white and black according to a definite proportion.

The Aristotelian doctrine of weight was one of the chief obstacles which seventeenth-century science had to contend with in establishing correct notions in dynamics. It is a curious feature of Greek science before Aristotle that, though the facts connected with gravity were well known, no one introduced the notion of weight to account for them. The difference between heavy bodies and light bodies had been previously treated as secondary for science. Plato's treatment of the matter is typical of the best fourth-century science. We must not try to explain why the heavier bodies tend to move towards the earth's surface by saying that they have a "downward" motion; their motion is not downward but "towards the centre" (the earth, though not fixed at the centre of the universe, being nearer to it than the rest of the solar and sidereal system). Plato then explains the tendency in virtue of which the heavier bodies move towards the "centre" as an attraction of like for like. The universal tendency is for smaller masses of "earth," "water," "air," "fire" to be attracted towards the great aggregations of the same materials. This is far from being a satisfactory theory in the light of facts which were not yet known to Plato, but it is on the right lines. It starts from the conception of the facts of gravity as due to an "attractive force" of some kind, and it has the great merit of bringing the "sinking" of stones and the "rising" of vapours under the same explanation.

Aristotle, though retaining the central idea that a body tends to move towards the region where the great cosmic mass of the same kind is congregated, introduced the entirely incompatible notion of an absolute distinction of "up" and "down." He identified the centre of the universe with that of the earth, and looked on motion to this centre as "downward." This led him to make a distinction between "heavy" bodies, which naturally tend to move "down," and "light" bodies, which tend to move "up" away from the centre. The doctrine works out thus. The heaviest elements tend to be massed together nearest the centre, the lightest to be furthest from it. Each element thus has its "proper place," that of water being immediately above earth, that of air next, and that of fire furthest from the centre, and nearest to the regions occupied by "celestial matter." (Readers of Dante will recollect the ascent from the Earthly Paradise through the "sphere of fire" with which the *Paradiso* opens.)

In its own "proper region" a body is simply quiescent; as we should say, any fluid loses its weight when immersed in itself. When a portion of an element is out of its own region and surrounded by the great cosmic aggregate of another element, either of two cases may occur. The body which is "out of its element" may be *below* its proper place, in which case it tends to move perpendicularly upwards to its place, or it may be *above* its proper place, and then it tends to move perpendicularly "down" until it reaches its place. Hence the two elements whose "proper place" is "below," earth and water, are absolutely heavy; those whose "proper place" is "above," air and fire, are light. It was this supposed real distinction between motion "up" and motion "down" which made it so hard for the contemporaries of Galileo to understand that an inflated bladder rises for the *same* reason that a stone sinks.

BIOLOGY

Of Aristotle's biology reasons of space forbid us to say much here. But a remark or two may be made about his theory of reproduction, since it is constantly referred to in much modern literature and has also played its part in theology. An interesting point is the distinction between "perfect" and "imperfect" animals. "Perfect" animals are those which can only be reproduced sexually. Aristotle held, however, that there are some creatures, even among vertebrates, which *may* be produced by the vivifying effect of solar heat on decomposing matter, without any parents at all. Thus malobservation of the facts of putrefaction led to the belief that flies and worms are engendered by heat from decaying bodies, and it was even thought that frogs and mice are produced in the same way from river-slime. In this process, the so-called "aequivocal generation," solar heat was conceived as the operative efficient cause which leads to the realisation of an organic "form" in the decaying matter.

In sexual reproduction Aristotle regards the male parent as the agent or efficient cause which contributes the element of form and organisation to the offspring. The female parent supplies only the raw material of the new creature, but she supplies the whole of this. No *material* is supplied by the male parent to the body of the offspring, a theory which St. Thomas found useful in defending the dogma of the Virgin Birth.

PSYCHOLOGY

Since the mind grows and develops, it comes under the class of things which have a "source of motion internal to themselves," and psychology is therefore, for Aristotle, a branch of Physics. To understand his treatment of psychological questions we need bear two things in mind. (1) *Psyche* or "soul" means in Greek more, and less, than "consciousness" does to us. Consciousness is a relatively late and highly developed manifestation of the principle which the Greeks call "soul." That principle shows itself not merely in consciousness but in the whole process of nutrition and growth and the adaptation of motor response to an external situation. Thus consciousness is a more secondary feature of the "soul" in Greek philosophy than in most modern thought, which has never ceased to be affected by Descartes' selection of "thought" as the special characteristic of psychical life. In common language the word *psyche* is constantly used where we should say "life" rather than "soul," and in Greek philosophy a work "on the *Psyche*" means what we should call one on "the principle of life."*

(2) It is a consequence of this way of thinking of the "soul" that the process of bodily and mental development is regarded by Aristotle as one single continuous process. The growth of a man's intellect and character by which he becomes a thinker and a citizen is a continuation of the process

---

* In particular the importance of self-consciousness is a discovery of the Neo-Platonist Plotinus.

by which his body is conceived and born and passes into physical manhood. This comes out in the words of the definition of the soul. "The soul is the first entelechy (or actual realisation) of a natural organic body." What this means is that the soul stands to the living body as all form realised in matter does to the matter of which it is the form, or that the soul is the "form" of the body. What the "organic body" is to the embryo out of which it has grown, that soul is to the body itself. As the embryo grows into the actual living body, so the living body grows into a body exhibiting the actual directing presence of mind. Aristotle illustrates the relation by the remark that if the whole body was one vast eye, sight would be its soul. As the eye is a tool for seeing with, but a living tool which is part of ourselves, so the body is a like tool or instrument for living with. Hence we may say of the soul that it is the "end" of the body, the activity to which the body is instrumental, as seeing is the "end" to which the eye is instrumental. But we must note that the soul is called only the "first" or initial "entelechy" of the body. The reason is that the mere presence of the soul does not guarantee the full living of the life to which our body is but the instrument. If we are to *live* in the fullest sense of the word, we must not merely "have" a soul; we "have" it even in sleep, in ignorance, in folly. The soul itself needs further to be educated and trained in intelligence and character, and to exercise its intelligence and character efficiently on the problems of thought and life. The mere "presence" of soul is only a first step in the progress towards fullness of life. This is why Aristotle calls the soul the *first* entelechy of the living body. The full and final entelechy is the life of intelligence and character actively functioning.

From this conception of the soul's relation to the body we see that Aristotle's "doctrine of body and mind" does not readily fall into line with any of the typical theories of our time. He neither thinks of the soul as a thing acting on the body and acted on by it, nor yet as a series of "states of mind" concomitant with certain "states of body." From his point of view to ask whether soul and body interact, or whether they exhibit "parallelism," would be much the same thing as to ask whether life interacts with the body, or whether there is a "parallelism" between vital processes and bodily processes. We must not ask at all how the body and soul are united. They are one thing, as the matter and the form of a copper globe are one. Thus they are in actual fact inseparable. The soul is the soul of its body and the body the body of its soul. We can only distinguish them by logical analysis, as we can distinguish the copper from the sphericity in the copper globe.

GRADES OF PSYCHICAL LIFE

If we consider the order of development, we find that some vital activities make their appearance earlier than others, and that it is a universal law that the more highly developed activities always have the less highly developed as their basis and precondition, though the less highly developed may exist apart from the more highly developed. So we may arrange vital activities in general in an ontogenetic order, the order in which they make their appearance in the individual's development. Aristotle reckons three such stages, the "nutritive," the "sensitive," and the "intelligent." The lowest form in which life shows itself at all, the level of minimum distinction between the living and the lifeless, is the power to take in nutriment, assimilate it, and grow. In vegetables the development is arrested at this point. With the animals we reach the next highest level, that of "sensitive" life. For all animals have at least the sense of touch.

Thus they all show sense-perception, and it is a consequence of this that they exhibit "appetition," the simplest form of conation, and the rudiments of feeling and "temper." For what has sensations can also feel pleasure and pain, and what can feel pleasure and pain can desire, since desire is only appetition of what is pleasant. Thus in the animals we have the beginnings of cognition, conation, and affective and emotional life in general. And Aristotle adds that locomotion makes its appearance at this level; animals do not, like plants, have to trust to their supply of nutriment coming to them; they can go to it.

The third level, that of "intelligence," *i.e.* the power to compare, calculate, and reflect, and to order one's life by conscious rule, is exhibited by man. What distinguishes life at this level from mere "sensitive" life is, on the intellectual side, the ability to cognise universal truths, on the conative, the power to live by rule instead of being swayed by momentary "appetition." The former gives us the possibility of science, the latter of moral excellence.*

SENSATION

Life manifests itself at the animal level on the cognitive side as sense-perception, on the conative as appetition or desire, on the affective as feeling of pleasure or pain, and in such simple emotional moods as "temper," resentment, longing. Aristotle gives sensation a logical priority over the conative and emotional expression of "animal" life. To experience appetition or anger or desire you must have an object which you crave for or desire or are angry with, and it is only when

* *Cf.* Dante's "Fatti non foste a viver come bruti,
  Ma per seguir virtute e conoscenza"
—that is, to follow practical (*virtute*) and speculative (*conoscenza*) reason.

you have reached the level of presentations through the senses that you can be said to have an object. Appetition or "temper" is as real a fact as perception, but you cannot crave for or feel angry with a thing you do not apprehend.

Aristotle's definition of sense-perception is that it is a "capacity for discerning" or distinguishing between "the sensible qualities of things." His conception of the process by which the discernment or distinguishing is effected is not altogether happy. In sense-perception the soul "takes into itself the *form* of the thing perceived without its *matter*, as sealing-wax receives the shape of an iron seal-ring without the iron." To understand this, we have to remember that for Aristotle the sensible qualities of the external world, colour, tones, tastes, and the rest, are not effects of mechanical stimulation of our sense-organs, but real qualities of bodies. The hardness of iron, the redness of a piece of red wax are all primarily "in" the iron or the wax. They are "forms," or determinations by definite law, of the "matter" of the iron or the wax. This will become clearer if we consider a definite example, the red colour of the wax. In the wax the red colour is a definite combination of the colour-opposites white and black according to a fixed ratio. Now Aristotle's view of the process of sense-perception is that when I become aware of the red colour the same proportion of white to black which makes the wax red is reproduced in my organ of vision; my eye, while I am seeing the red, "assimilated" to the wax, is itself for the time actually "reddened." But it does not become *wax* although the red thing I am looking at is a piece of red *wax*. The eye remains a thing composed of living tissues. This is what is meant by saying that in seeing the colours of things the eye receives "forms" without the "matter" of the things in which those forms are exhibited. Thus the process of sense-perception is one in which the organ of sense is temporarily assimilated to the thing apprehended in respect of the particular quality cognised by that organ, but in respect of no other. According to Aristotle this process of "assimilation" always requires the presence of a "medium." If an object is in immediate contact with the eye we cannot see its colour; if it is too near the ear, we do not discern the note it gives out. Even in the case of touch and taste there is no immediate contact between the object perceived and the true organ of perception. For in touch the "flesh" is not the organ of apprehension but an integument surrounding it and capable of acting as an intermediary between it and things. Thus perception is always accomplished by a "motion" set up in the "medium" by the external object, and by the medium in our sense-organs. Aristotle thus contrives to bring correct apprehension by sense of the qualities of things under the formula of the "right mean" or "right proportion," which is better known from the use made of it in the philosopher's theory of conduct. The colour of a surface, the pitch of the note given out by a vibrating string, etc., depend on, and vary with, certain forms or ratios "in" the surface or the vibrating string; our correct apprehension of the qualities depends on the reproduction of the *same* ratios in our sense-organs, the establishment of the "right proportion" in *us*. That this "right proportion" may be reproduced in our own sense-organs it is necessary (1) that the medium should have none of the sensible qualities for the apprehension whereof it serves as medium, *e.g.* the medium in colour-perception must be colourless. If it had a colour of its own, the "motion" set up by the coloured bodies we apprehend would not be transmitted undistorted to our organs; we should see everything through a coloured haze. It is necessary for the same reason (2) that the percipient organ itself, when in a state of quiescence, should possess none of the qualities which can be induced in it by stimulation. The upshot of the whole theory is that the sense-organ is "potentially" what the sense-quality it apprehends is actually. Actual perceiving is just that special transition from the potential to the actual which results in making the organ for the time being *actually* of the same quality as the object.

THE COMMON SENSIBLES AND THE COMMON SENSE-ORGAN

Every sense has a range of qualities connected with it as its special objects. Colours can only be perceived by the eye, sounds by the ear, and so forth. But there are certain characters of perceived things which we appear to apprehend by more than one sense. Thus we seem to perceive size and shape either by touch or by sight, and number by hearing as well, since we can count *e.g.* the strokes of an unseen bell. Hence Aristotle distinguishes between the "special sensible qualities" such as colour and pitch, and what he calls the "common sensibles," the characters of things which can be perceived by more than one organ. These are enumerated as size, form or shape, number, motion (and its opposite rest), being. (The addition of this last is, of course, meant to account for our conviction that any perceived colour, taste, or other quality *is* a reality and not a delusion.) The list corresponds very closely with one given by Plato of the "things which the mind perceives *by herself without the help of any organ,*" *i.e.* of the leading determinations of sensible things which are due not to sense but to understanding. It was an unfortunate innovation to regard the discernment of number or movement, which obviously demand intellectual processes such as counting and comparison, as performed immediately by "sense," and to assign the apprehension of number, movement, figure to a central "organ." This organ he finds in the heart. The theory is that when the "special organs" of the senses are stimulated, they in turn communicate movements to the blood and "animal spirits" (*i.e.* the vapours supposed to be produced from the blood by animal heat). These movements are propagated inwards to the heart, where they all meet. This is supposed to account for the important fact that, though our sensations are so many and diverse, we are conscious of our own unity as the subjects apprehending all this variety. The unity of the perceiving subject is thus made to depend on the unity of the ultimate "organ of sensation," the heart. Further, when once a type of motion has been set up in any sense-organ at the periphery of the body it will be propagated inward to the "common sensorium" in the heart. The motions set up by stimulation, *e.g.* of the eye and of the skin, are partly different, partly the same (viz. in so far as they are determined by the number, shape, size, movement of the external stimuli). Hence in the heart itself the stimulation on which perception of number or size depends is one and the same whether it has been transmitted from the eye or from the skin. Awareness of lapse of time is also regarded as a function of the "common sense-organ," since it is the "common sensory" which perceives motion, and lapse of time is apprehended only in the apprehension of motion. Thus, in respect of the inclusion of geometrical form and lapse of time among the "common sensibles," there is a certain resemblance between Aristotle's doctrine and Kant's theory that recognition of spatial and temporal order is a function not of understanding but of "pure" sense. It is further held that to be aware that one is perceiving (self-consciousness) and to discriminate between the different classes of "special" sense-perception must also be functions of the "common sense-organ." Thus Aristotle makes the mistake of treating the most fundamental acts of intelligent reflection as precisely on a par, from the point of view of the theory of knowledge, with awareness of colour or sound.

A more legitimate function assigned to the "common sensorium" in the heart is that "fantasy," the formation of mental imagery, depends on its activity. The simplest kind of "image," the pure memory-image left behind after the object directly arousing perception has ceased to stimulate, is due to the persistence of the movements set up in the heart after the sensory process in the peripheral organ is over. Since Aristotle denies the possibility of thinking without the aid of memory-images, this function of the "common sensorium" is the indispensable basis of mental recall, anticipation, and thought. Neither "experience," *i.e.* a general conviction which results from the frequent repetition of similar perceptions, nor thought can arise in any animal in which sense-stimulation does not leave such "traces" behind it. Similarly "free imagery," the existence of trains of imagination not tied down to the reproduction of an actual order of sensations, is accounted for by the consideration that "chance coincidence" may lead to the stimulation of the heart in the same way in which it might have been stimulated by actual sensation-processes. Sleeping and waking and the experiences of dream-life are likewise due to changes in the functioning of the "common sense-organ," brought about partly by fatigue in the superficial sense-organs, partly by qualitative changes in the blood and "animal spirits" caused by the processes of nutrition and digestion. Probably Aristotle's best scientific work in psychology is contained in the series of small essays in which this theory of memory and its imagery is worked out. (Aristotle's language about the "common sensibles" is, of course, the source of our expression "common sense," which, however, has an entirely different meaning. The shifting of sense has apparently been effected through Cicero's employment of the phrase *sensus communis* to mean tactful sympathy, the feeling of fellowship with our kind on which the Stoic philosophers laid so much stress.)

THOUGHT

Though thinking is impossible except by the use of imagery, to think is not merely to possess trains of imagery, or even to be aware of possessing them. Thinking means understanding the *meaning* of such mental imagery and arriving through the understanding at knowledge of the structure of the real world. How this process of interpreting mental imagery and reaching truth is achieved with greater and greater success until it culminates in the apprehension of the supreme principles of philosophy we have seen in dealing with the Aristotelian theory of knowledge. From the point of view of the "physicist" who is concerned with thinking simply as a type of natural process, the relation of "understanding" to the mental imagery just described is analogous to that of sensation to sensible qualities. The objects which thinking apprehends are the universal types of relation by which the world of things is pervaded. The process of thinking is one in which this system of universal relations is reproduced "by way of idea" in the mind of the thinker. The "understanding" thus stands to its objects as matter to form. The process of getting actually to understand the world is one in which our "thought" or "understanding" steadily receives completer determination and "form" from its contemplation of reality. In this sense, the process is one in which the understanding may be said to be passive in knowledge. It is passive because it is the subject which, at every fresh stage in the progress to knowledge, is being quite literally "informed" by the action of the real world through the sensation and imagery. Hence Aristotle says that, in order that the understanding may be correctly "informed" by its contact with its objects, it must, before the process begins, have no determinate character of its own. It must be simply a capacity for apprehending the types of interconnection. "What is called the intelligence—I mean that with which the soul thinks and understands—is not an actual thing until it thinks." (This is meant to exclude any doctrine which credits the "understanding" with either *furniture* of its own such as "innate ideas," or a specific *structure* of its own. If the results of our thinking arose partly from the structure of the world of objects and partly from inherent laws of the "structure of mind," our thought at its best would not reproduce the universal "forms" or "types" of interconnection as they really are, but would distort them, as the shapes of things are distorted when we see them through a lens of high refractive index.) Thus, though Aristotle differs from the modern empiricists in holding that "universals" really exist "in" things, and are the links of connection between them, he agrees with the empiricist that knowledge is not the resultant of a combination of "facts" on the one side and "fundamental laws of the mind's working" on the other. At the outset the "understanding" has *no* structure; it develops a structure for itself in the same process, and to the same degree, in which it apprehends the "facts." Hence the "understanding" only is real in the actual process of understanding its objects, and again in a sense the understanding and the things it understands are one. Only we must qualify this last statement by saying that it is only "potentially" that the understanding *is* the forms which it apprehends. Aristotle does not mean by this that such things as horses and oxen are thoughts or "ideas." By the things with which "understanding" is said to be one he means the "forms" which we apprehend when we actually understand the world or any part of it, the truths of science. His point then is that the actual thinking of these truths and the truths themselves do not exist apart from one another. "Science" does not mean certain things written down in a book; it means a mind engaged in thinking and knowing things, and of the mind itself, considered out of its relation to the actual life of thinking the truths of science, we can say no more than that it is a name for the fact that we are capable of achieving such thought.

THE ACTIVE INTELLIGENCE

So far Aristotle's account of thought has been plain sailing. Thought has been considered as the final and highest development of the vital functions of the organism, and hence as something inseparable from the lower functions of nutrition and sensitive life. The existence of a thought which is not a function of a living body, and which is not "passive," has been absolutely excluded. But at this point we are suddenly met by the most startling of all the inconsistencies between the naturalistic and the "spiritualist" strains in Aristotle's philosophy. In a few broken lines he tells us that there is another sense of the word "thought" in which "thought" actually creates the truths it understands, just as light may be said to make the colours which we see by its aid. "And *this* intelligence," he adds, "is separable from matter, and impassive and unmixed, being in its essential nature an *activity*. . . . It has no intermission in its thinking. It is only in separation from matter that it is fully itself, and it alone is immortal and everlasting . . . while the passive intelligence is perishable and does not think at all, apart from this." The meaning of this is not made clear by Aristotle himself, and the interpretation was disputed even among the philosopher's personal disciples.

One important attempt to clear up the difficulty is that made by Alexander of Aphrodisias, the greatest of the commentators on Aristotle, in the second century A.D. Alexander said, as Aristotle had not done, that the "active intelligence" is numerically the same in all men, and is identical with God. Thus, all that is specifically human in each of us is the "passive intelligence" or capacity for being enlightened by God's activity upon us. The advantage of the view is, that it removes the "active intelligence" altogether from the purview of psychology, which then becomes a purely naturalistic science. The great Arabian Aristotelian, Averroes (Ibn Roshd) of Cordova, in the twelfth century, went still further in the direction of naturalism. Since the "active" and "passive" intelligence can only be separated by a logical abstraction, he inferred that men, speaking strictly, do not think at all; there is only one and the same individual intelligence in the universe, and all that we call our thinking is really not ours but God's. The great Christian scholastics of the following century in general read Aristotle through the eyes of Averroes, "*the* Commentator," as St. Thomas calls him, "Averrois che il gran commento feo," as Dante says. But their theology compelled them to disavow his doctrine of the "active intelligence," against which they could also bring, as St. Thomas does, the telling argument that Aristotle could never have meant to say that there really is no such thing as *human* intelligence. Hence arose a third interpretation, the Thomist, according to which the "active intelligence" is neither God nor the same for all men, but is the highest and most rational "part" of the individual human soul, which has no bodily "organ." Aristotle had said of it that it is the only thing in us which is not contributed by our parents, but comes "from outside." In Christian theology this becomes the doctrine that the "rational soul" is directly created by God.

87

V

PRACTICAL PHILOSOPHY

HITHERTO
we have been concerned with the speculative branches of
knowledge; we have now to turn to practice. Practice, too,
is an activity of thought, but an activity which is never
satisfied by the process of thinking itself. In practice our
thinking is always directed towards the production of some
result other than true thought itself. As in engineering it is
not enough to find a solution of the problem how to build
a bridge over a given river capable of sustaining a given
strain, so in directing our thought on the problems of
human conduct and the organisation of society we aim at
something more than the understanding of human life. In
the one case what we aim at is the construction of the bridge;
in the other it is the production of goodness in ourselves and
our fellow-men, and the establishment of right social
relations in the state. Aristotle is careful to insist on this point
throughout his whole treatment of moral and social problems. The principal object of his lectures on conduct is not to
tell his hearers what goodness is, but to make them good,
and similarly it is quite plain that *Politics* was intended as a
text-book for legislators. In close connection with this
practical object stands his theory of the kind of truth which

must be looked for in ethics and politics. He warns us against expecting precepts which have the exact and universal rigidity of the truths of speculative science. Practical science has to do with the affairs of men's lives, matters which are highly complex and variable, in a word, with "what may be otherwise." Hence we must be content if we can lay down precepts which hold good in the main, just as in medicine we do not expect to find prescriptions which will effect a cure in all cases, but are content with general directions which require to be adapted to special cases by the experience and judgment of the practitioner. The object of practical science then is to formulate rules which will guide us in obtaining our various ends. Now when we consider these ends we see at once that some are subordinate to others. The manufacture of small-arms may be the end at which their maker aims, but it is to the military man a mere means to *his* end, which is the effective use of them. Successful use of arms is again the end of the professional soldier, but it is a mere means among others to the statesman. Further, it is the military men who use the arms from whom the manufacturer has to take his directions as to the kind of arms that are wanted, and again it is the statesman to whom the professional soldiers have to look for directions as to when and with what general objects in view they shall fight. So the art which uses the things produced by another art is the superior and directing art; the art which makes the things, the inferior and subordinate art. Hence the supreme practical art is politics, since it is the art which uses the products turned out by all other arts as means to its ends. It is the business of politics, the art of the statesman, to prescribe to the practitioners of all other arts and professions the lines on which and the conditions under which they shall exercise their vocation with a view to securing the supreme practical end, the well-being of the community. Among the other professions and arts which make the materials the statesman employs, the profession of the educator stands foremost. The statesman is bound to demand certain qualities of mind and character in the individual citizens. The production of these mental and moral qualities must therefore be the work of the educator. It thus becomes an important branch of politics to specify the kind of mental and moral qualities which a statesman should require the educator to produce in his pupils.

It is this branch of politics which Aristotle discusses in his *Ethics*. He never contemplates a study of the individual's good apart from politics, the study of the good of the society. What then is the good or the best kind of life for an individual member of society? Aristotle answers that as far as the mere name is concerned, there is a general agreement to call the best life, *Eudaimonia*, Happiness. But the real problem is one of fact. What kind of life deserves to be called happiness? Plato had laid it down that the happy life must satisfy three conditions. It must be desirable for its own sake, it must be sufficient of itself to satisfy us, and it must be the life a wise man would prefer to any other. The question is, What general formula can we find which will define the life that satisfies these conditions? To find the answer we have to consider what Plato and Aristotle call the work or function of man. By the work of anything we mean what can only be done by it, or by it better than by anything else. Thus the work of the eye is to see. You cannot see with any other organ, and when the eye does this work of seeing well you say it is a good eye. So we may say of any living being that its work is to live, and that it is a good being when it does this work of living efficiently. To do its own work efficiently is the excellence or virtue of the thing. The excellence or virtue of a man will thus be to live efficiently, but since life can be manifested at different levels, if we would know what man's work is we must ask whether there is not some form of life which can *only* be lived by man. Now the life which consists in merely feeding and growing belongs to all organisms and can be lived with equal vigour by them all. There is, however, a kind of life which can only be lived by man—the life which consists in conscious direction of one's actions by a rule. It is the work of man to live this kind of life, and his happiness consists in living it efficiently and well. So we may give as the definition of human well-being that it is "an active life in accord with excellence, or if there are more forms of excellence than one, in accord with the best and completest of them"; and we must add "in a complete life" to show that mere promise not crowned by performance does not suffice to entitle man's life to be called happy. We can see that this definition satisfies Plato's three conditions. A vigorous and active living in a way which calls into play the specifically human capacities of man is desirable for its own sake, and preferable to any other life which could be proposed to us. It too is the only life which can permanently satisfy men, but we must add that if such a life is to be lived adequately certain advantages of fortune must be presupposed. We cannot fully live a life of this kind if we are prevented from exercising our capacities by lack of means or health or friends and associates, and even the calamities which arise in the course of events may be so crushing as to hinder a man, for a time, from putting forth his full powers. These external good things are not constituents of happiness, but merely necessary conditions of that exercise of our own capacities which is the happy life.

In our definition of the happy life we said that it was one of activity in accord with goodness or excellence, and we left it an open question whether there are more kinds of such goodness than one. On consideration we see that two kinds of goodness or excellence are required in living the happy life. The happy life for man is a life of conscious following of a rule. To live it well, then, you need to know what the right rule to follow is, and you need also to follow it. There are persons who deliberately follow a wrong rule of life—the wicked. There are others who know what the right rule is but fail to follow it because their tempers and appetites are unruly—the morally weak. To live the happy life, then, two sorts of goodness are required. You must have a good judgment as to what the right rule is (or if you cannot find it out for yourself, you must at least be able to recognise it when it is laid down by someone else, the teacher or lawgiver), and you must have your appetites, feelings, and emotions generally so trained that they obey the rule. Hence excellence, goodness, or virtue is divided into goodness of intellect and goodness of character (*moral* goodness), the word *character* being used for the complex of tempers, feelings, and the affective side of human nature generally. In education goodness of character has to be produced by training and discipline before goodness of intellect can be imparted. The young generally have to be trained to obey the right rule before they can see for themselves that it is the right rule, and if a man's tempers and passions are not first schooled into actual obedience to the rule he will in most cases never see that it is the right rule at all. Hence Aristotle next goes on to discuss the general character of the kind of goodness he calls goodness of character, the right state of the feelings and passions.

The first step towards understanding what goodness of character is is to consider the way in which it is actually produced. We are not born with this goodness of tempers and feelings ready made, nor yet do we obtain it by theoretical instruction; it is a result of a training and discipline of the feelings and impulses. The possibility of such a training is due to the fact that feelings and impulses are rational capacities, and a rational capacity can be developed into either of two contrasted activities according to the training it receives. You cannot train stones to fall upwards, but you can train a hot temper to display itself either in the form of righteous resentment of wrong-doing or in that of violent defiance of all authority. Our natural emotions and impulses are in themselves neither good nor bad; they are the raw material out of which training makes good or bad character according to the direction it gives to them. The effect of training is to convert the indeterminate tendency into a fixed habit. We may say, then, that moral goodness is a fixed state of the soul produced by habituation. By being trained in habits of endurance, self-mastery, and fair dealing, we acquire the kind of character to which it is pleasing to act bravely, continently, and fairly, and disagreeable to act unfairly, profligately, or like a coward. When habituation has brought about this result the moral excellences in question have become part of our inmost self and we are in full possession of goodness of character. In a word, it is by repeated doing of right acts that we acquire the right kind of character.

But what general characteristics distinguish right acts and right habits from wrong ones? Aristotle is guided in answering the question by an analogy which is really at the bottom of all Greek thinking on morality. The thought is that goodness is in the soul what health and fitness are in the body, and that the preceptor is for the soul what the physician or the trainer is for the body. Now it was a well-known medical theory, favoured by both Plato and Aristotle, that health in the body means a condition of balance or equilibration among the elements of which it is composed. When the hot and the cold, the moist and the dry in the composition of the human frame exactly balance one another, the body is in perfect health. Hence the object of

93

the regimen of the physician or the trainer is to produce and maintain a proper balance or proportion between the ingredients of the body. Any course which disturbs this balance is injurious to health and strength. You damage your health if you take too much food or exercise, and also if you take too little. The same thing is true of health in the soul. Our soul's health may be injured by allowing too much or too little play to any of our natural impulses or feelings. We may lay it down, then, that the kind of training which gives rise to a good habit is training in the avoidance of the opposite errors of the too much and the too little. And since the effect of training is to produce habits which issue in the spontaneous performance of the same kind of acts by which the habits were acquired, we may say not merely that goodness of character is produced by acts which exhibit a proper balance or mean, but that it *is* a settled habit of acting so as to exhibit the same balance or proportion. Hence the formal definition of goodness of character is that it is "a settled condition of the soul which wills or chooses the mean relatively to ourselves, this mean being determined by a rule or whatever we like to call that by which the wise man determines it."

There are several points in this definition of the mean upon which moral virtue depends of which we must take note unless we are to misunderstand Aristotle seriously. To begin with, the definition expressly says that "moral goodness is a state of will or choice." Thus it is not enough that one should follow the rule of the mean outwardly in one's actions; one's personal will must be regulated by it. Goodness of character is inward; it is not merely outward. Next we must not suppose that Aristotle means that the "just enough" is the same for all our feelings, that every impulse has a moral right to the same authority in shaping our conduct as any other. How much or how little is the just enough in connection with a given spring of action is one of the things which the wise man's rule has to determine, just as the wise physician's rule may determine that a very little quantity is the just enough in the case of some articles of diet or curative drugs, while in the case of others the just enough may be a considerable amount. Also the right mean is not the same for every one. What we have to attain is the mean relatively to *ourselves*, and this will be different for persons of different constitutions and in different conditions. It is this relativity of the just enough to the individual's personality and circumstances which makes it impossible to lay down precise rules of conduct applicable alike to everybody, and renders the practical attainment of goodness so hard. It is my duty to spend some part of my income in taking a yearly holiday, but no general rule will tell me what percentage of my income is the right amount for me to spend in this way. That depends on a host of considerations, such as the excess of my income above my necessary expenses and the like. Or again, the just enough may vary with the same man according to the circumstances of the particular case. No rule of thumb application of a formula will decide such problems. Hence Aristotle insists that the right mean in the individual case has always to be determined by immediate insight. This is precisely why goodness of intellect needs to be added to goodness of character. His meaning is well brought out by an illustration which I borrow from Professor Burnet. "On a given occasion there will be a temperature which is just right for my morning bath. If the bath is hotter than this, it will be too hot; if it is colder, it will be too cold. But as this just right temperature varies with the condition of my body, it cannot be ascertained by simply using a thermometer. If I am in good general health I shall, however, know by the feel of the water when the temperature is right. So if I am in good moral health I shall know, without appealing to a formal code of maxims, what is the right degree, *e.g.* of indignation to show in a given case, how it should be shown and towards whom." Thus we see why Aristotle demands goodness of character as a preliminary condition of goodness of intellect or judgment in moral matters. Finally, if we ask by *what* rule the mean is determined, the answer will be that the rule is the judgment of the legislator who determines what is the right mean by his knowledge of the conditions on which the well-being of the community depends. He then embodies his insight in the laws which he makes and the regulations he imposes on the educators of youth. The final aim of education in goodness is to make our immediate judgment as to what is right coincide with the spirit of a wise legislation.

The introduction of the reference to will or choice into the definition of goodness of character leads Aristotle to consider the relation of will to conduct. His main object is to escape the paradoxical doctrine which superficial students might derive from the works of Plato, that wrong-doing is always well-meaning ignorance. Aristotle's point is that it is the condition of will revealed by men's acts which is the real object of our approval or blame. This is because in voluntary action the man himself is the efficient cause of his act. Hence the law recognises only two grounds on which a man may plead that he is not answerable for what he does. (1) Actual physical compulsion by *force majeure*. (2) Ignorance, not due to the man's own previous negligence, of some circumstances material to the issue. When either of these pleas can be made with truth the man does not really contribute by his choice to the resulting act, and therefore is not really its cause. But a plea of ignorance of the general laws of morality does not excuse. I cannot escape responsibility for a murder by pleading that I did not know that murder is wrong. Such a plea does not exempt me from having been

96

the cause of the murder; it only shows that my moral principles are depraved.

More precisely will is a process which has both an intellectual and an appetitive element. The appetitive element is our wish for some result. The intellectual factor is the calculation of the steps by which that result may be obtained. When we wish for the result we begin to consider how it might be brought about, and we continue our analysis until we find that the chain of conditions requisite may be started by the performance of some act now in our power to do. Will may thus be defined as the deliberate appetition of something within our power, and the very definition shows that our choice is an efficient cause of the acts we choose to do. This is why we rightly regard men as responsible or answerable for their acts of choice, good and bad alike.

From the analysis of goodness of character we proceed to that of goodness of intellect. The important point is to decide which of all the forms of goodness of intellect is that which must be combined with goodness of character to make a man fit to be a citizen of the state. It must be a kind of intellectual excellence which makes a man see what the right rule by which the mean is determined is. Now when we come to consider the different excellences of intellect we find that they all fall under one of two heads, theoretical or speculative wisdom and practical wisdom.

Theoretical wisdom is contained in the sciences which give us universal truths about the fixed and unalterable relations of the things in the universe, or, as we should say, which teach us the laws of Nature. Its method is syllogism, the function of which is to make us see how the more complex truths are implied in simpler principles. Practical wisdom is intelligence as employed in controlling and directing human life to the production of the happy life for a community, and it is this form of intellectual excellence which we require of the statesman. It is required of him not only that he should know in general what things are good for man, but also that he should be able to judge correctly that in given circumstances such and such an act is the one which will secure the good. He must not only know the right rule itself, which corresponds to the major premiss of syllogism in theoretical science, but he must understand the character of particular acts so as to see that they fall under the right rule. Thus the method of practical wisdom will be analogous to that of theoretical wisdom. In both cases what we have to do is to see that certain special facts are cases of a general law or rule. Hence Aristotle calls the method of practical wisdom the practical syllogism or syllogism of action, since its peculiarity is that what issues from the putting together of the premisses is not an assertion but the performance of an act. In the syllogism of action, the conclusion, that is to say, the performance of a given act, just as in the syllogism of theory, is connected with the rule given in the major premiss by a statement of fact; thus *e.g.* the performance of a specific act such as the writing of this book is connected with the general rule that what helps to spread knowledge ought to be done by the conviction that the writing of this book helps to spread knowledge. Our perception of such a fact is like a sense-perception in its directness and immediacy. We see therefore that the kind of intellectual excellence which the statesman must possess embraces at once a right conception of the general character of the life which is best for man, because it calls into play his specific capacities as a human being, and also a sound judgment in virtue of which he sees correctly that particular acts are expressions of this good for man. This, then, is what we mean by practical wisdom.

So far, then, it would seem that the best life for man is just the life of co-operation in the life of the State, which man, being the only political animal or animal capable of life in a State, has as his peculiar work, and as if the end of all moral education should be to make us good and efficient citizens. But in the *Ethics*, as elsewhere, the end of Aristotle's argument has a way of forgetting the beginning. We find that there is after all a still higher life open to man than that of public affairs. Affairs and business of all kinds are only undertaken as means to getting leisure, just as civilised men go to war, not for the love of war itself, but to secure peace. The highest aim of life, then, is not the carrying on of political business for its own sake, but the worthy and noble employment of leisure, the periods in which we are our own masters. It has the advantage that it depends more purely on ourselves and our own internal resources than any other life of which we know, for it needs very little equipment with external goods as compared with any form of the life of action. It calls into play the very highest of our own capacities as intelligent beings, and for that very reason the active living of it is attended with the purest of all pleasures. In it, moreover, we enter at intervals and for a little while, so far as the conditions of our mundane existence allow, into the life which God enjoys through an unbroken eternity. Thus we reach the curious paradox that while the life of contemplation is said to be that of our truest self, it is also maintained that this highest and happiest life is one which we live, not in respect of being human, but in respect of having a divine something in us. When we ask what this life of contemplation includes, we see from references in the *Politics* that it includes the genuinely aesthetic appreciation of good literature and music and pictorial and plastic art, but there can be no doubt that what bulks most largely in Aristotle's mind is the active pursuit of science for its own sake, particularly of such studies as First Philosophy and Physics, which deal with the fundamental structure of the universe. Aristotle thus definitely ends by placing the life of the scholar and the student on the very summit of felicity.

It is from this doctrine that mediaeval Christianity derives its opposition between the *vita contemplativa* and *vita activa* and its preference for the former, though in the mediaeval mind the contemplative life has come to mean generally a kind of brooding over theological speculations and of absorption in mystical ecstasy very foreign to the spirit of Aristotle. The types by which the contrast of the two lives is illustrated—Rachel and Leah, Mary and Martha—are familiar to all readers of Christian literature.

THE THEORY OF THE STATE

Man is by nature a political animal, a being who can only develop his capacities by sharing in the life of a community. Hence Aristotle definitely rejects the view that the State or Society is a mere creature of convention or agreement, an institution made by compact between individuals for certain special ends, not growing naturally out of the universal demands and aspirations of humanity. Mankind, he urges, have never existed at all as isolated individuals. Some rudimentary form of social organisation is to be found wherever men are to be found. The actual stages in the development of social organisation have been three—the family, the village community, the city State. In the very rudest forms of social life known to us, the patriarchal family, not the individual, is the social unit. Men lived at first in separate families under the control of the head of the family. Now a family is made up in its simplest form of at least three persons—a man, his wife, and a servant or slave to do the hard work; though very poor men often have to replace the servant by an ox as the drudge of all work. Children when they come swell the number, and thus we see the beginnings of complex social relations of subordination in the family itself. It involves three such distinct relations, that of husband and wife, that of parent and child, that of master and man. The family passes into the village community, partly by the tendency of several families of common descent to remain together under the direction of the oldest male member of the group, partly by the association of a number of distinct families for purposes of mutual help and protection against common dangers. Neither of these forms of association, however, makes adequate provision for the most permanent needs of human nature. Complete security for a permanent supply of material necessaries and adequate protection only come when a number of such scattered communities pool their resources, and surround themselves with a city wall. The city State, which has come into being in this way, proves adequate to provide from its own internal resources for all the spiritual as well as the material needs of its members. Hence the independent city State does not grow as civilisation advances into any higher form of organisation, as the family and village grew into it. It is the end, the last word of social progress. It is amazing to us that this piece of cheap conservatism should have been uttered at the very time when the system of independent city States had visibly broken down, and a former pupil of Aristotle himself was founding a gigantic empire to take their place as the vehicle of civilisation.

The end for which the State exists is not merely its own self-perpetuation. As we have seen, Aristotle assigns a higher value to the life of the student than to the life of practical affairs. Since it is only in the civilised State that the student can pursue his vocation, the ultimate reason for which the State exists is to educate its citizens in such a way as shall fit them to make the noble use of leisure. In the end the State itself is a means to the spiritual cultivation of its individual members. This implies that the chosen few, who have a vocation to make full use of the opportunities provided for leading this life of noble leisure, are the real end for the sake of which society exists. The other citizens who have no qualification for any life higher than that of business and affairs are making the most of themselves in devoting their lives to the conduct and maintenance of the organisation whose full advantages they are unequal to share in. It is from this point of view also that Aristotle treats the social problem of the existence of a class whose whole life is spent in doing the hard work of society, and thus setting the citizen body free to make the best use it can of leisure. In the conditions of life in the Greek world this class consisted mainly of slaves, and thus the problem Aristotle has to face is the moral justifiability of slavery. We must remember that he knew slavery only in its comparatively humane Hellenic form. The slaves of whom he speaks were household servants and assistants in small businesses. He had not before his eyes the system of enormous industries carried on by huge gangs of slaves under conditions of revolting degradation which disgraced the later Roman Republic and the early Roman Empire, or the Southern States of North America. His problems are in all essentials much the same as those which concern us to-day in connection with the social position of the classes who do the hard bodily work of the community. As against social revolutionaries who regard all slavery as wrong, Aristotle holds that it would certainly be wrong if it meant the condemnation of the slave to a worse life than the best of which he is capable. But it does not really mean this. Non-Greeks, "barbarians," do not really possess the capacity for being their own masters or for living either the life of the civilised man of affairs or that of the student. They attain the highest mental and moral development of which they are capable, not when left in their native "barbarism," but when they occupy the position of servants in a civilised Greek society. A Thracian who is the slave of a decent and kindly Greek master is living a worthier life than a Thracian who runs wild on his "native heath." It is thus really for his own good and for his own happiness that he should make the best of himself; he is not wronged by losing a "freedom" of which he is incapable of making the proper use. Much in the same way evangelical Protestants used at one time to defend negro slavery in our own colonies by the plea that the slave got opportunities of salvation which he could not have enjoyed as a free heathen in his native Africa.

Much consideration is given in the *Politics* to the classification of the different types of constitution possible for the city State. The current view was that there are three main types, distinguished by the number of persons who form the sovereign political authority: monarchy, in which sovereign power belongs to a single person; oligarchy, in which it is in the hands of a select few; democracy, in which it is enjoyed by the whole body of the citizens. Aristotle observes, correctly, that the really fundamental distinction between a Greek oligarchy and a Greek democracy was that the former was government by the propertied classes, the latter government by the masses. Hence the watchword of democracy was always that all political rights should belong equally to all citizens; that of oligarchy, that a man's political status should be graded according to his "stake in the country." Both ideals are, according to him, equally mistaken, since the real end of government, which both overlook, is the promotion of the "good life." In a State which recognises this ideal, an aristocracy or government by the best, only the "best" men will possess the full rights of citizenship, whether they are many or few. There might even be a monarch at the head of such a State, if it happened to contain some one man of outstanding intellectual and moral worth. Such a State should be the very opposite of a great imperial power. It should, that its cultivation may be the more intensive, be as small as is compatible with complete independence of outside communities for its material and spiritual sustenance, and its territory should only be large enough to provide its members with the permanent possibility of ample leisure, so long as they are content with plain and frugal living. Though it ought not, for military and other reasons, to be cut off from communication with the sea, the great military and commercial highroad of the Greek world, it ought not to be near enough to the coast to run any risk of imperilling its moral cultivation by becoming a great emporium, like the Athens of Pericles. In the organisation of the society care should be taken to exclude the agricultural and industrial population from full citizenship, which carries with it the right to appoint and to be appointed as administrative magistrates. This is because these classes, having no opportunity for the worthy employment of leisure, cannot be trusted to administer the State for the high ends which it is its true function to further.

Thus Aristotle's political ideal is that of a small but leisured and highly cultivated aristocracy, without large fortunes or any remarkable differences in material wealth, free from the spirit of adventure and enterprise, pursuing the arts and sciences quietly while its material needs are supplied by the labour of a class excluded from citizenship, kindly treated but without prospects. Weimar, in the days when Thackeray knew it as a lad, would apparently reproduce the ideal better than any other modern State one can think of.

The object of the *Politics* is, however, not merely to discuss the ideal State, but to give practical advice to men who might be looking forward to actual political life, and would therefore largely have to be content with making the best of existing institutions. In the absence of the ideal aristocracy, Aristotle's preference is for what he calls Polity or constitutional government, a sort of compromise between oligarchy and democracy in which political power is in the hands of the "middle" classes. Of course a practical statesman may have to work with a theoretically undesirable constitution, such as an oligarchy or an unqualified democracy. But it is only in an ideal constitution that the education which makes its subject a good man, in the philosopher's sense of the word, will also make him a good citizen. If the constitution is bad, then the education best fitted to make a man loyal to it may have to be very different from that which you would choose to make him a good man. The discussion of the kind of education desirable for the best kind of State, in which to be a loyal citizen and to be a good man are the same thing, is perhaps the most permanently valuable part of the *Politics*. Though Aristotle's writings on "practical" philosophy have been more read in modern times than any other part of his works, they are far from being his best and most thorough performances. In no department of his thought is he quite so slavishly dependent on his master Plato as in the theory of the "good for man" and the character of "moral" excellence. No Aristotelian work is quite so commonplace in its handling of a vast subject as the *Politics*. In truth his interest in these social questions is not of the deepest. He is, in accordance with his view of the superiority of "theoretical science," entirely devoid of the spirit of the social reformer. What he really cares about is "theology" and "physics," and the fact that the objects of the educational regulations of the *Politics* are all designed to encourage the study of these "theoretical" sciences, makes this section of the *Politics* still one of the most valuable expositions of the aims and requirements of a "liberal" education.

All education must be under public control, and education

must be universal and compulsory. Public control is necessary, not merely to avoid educational anarchy, but because it is a matter of importance to the community that its future citizens should be trained in the way which will make them most loyal to the constitution and the ends it is designed to subserve. Even in one of the "bad" types of State, where the life which the constitution tends to foster is not the highest, the legislator's business is to see that education is directed towards fostering the "spirit of the constitution." There is to be an "atmosphere" which impregnates the whole of the teaching, and it is to be an "atmosphere" of public spirit. The only advantage which Aristotle sees in private education is that it allows of more modification of programme to meet the special needs of the individual pupil than a rigid State education which is to be the same for all. The actual regulations which Aristotle lays down are not very different from those of Plato. Both philosophers hold that "primary" education, in the early years of life, should aim partly at promoting bodily health and growth by a proper system of physical exercises, partly at influencing character and giving a refined and elevated tone to the mind by the study of letters, art, and music. Both agree that this should be followed in the later "teens" by two or three years of specially rigorous systematic military training combined with a taste of actual service in the less exhausting and less dangerous parts of a soldier's duty. It is only after this, at about the age at which young men now take a "university" course, that Plato and Aristotle would have the serious scientific training of the intellect begun. The *Politics* leaves the subject just at the point where the young men are ready to undergo their special military training. Thus we do not know with certainty what scientific curriculum Aristotle would have recommended, though we may safely guess that it would have contained comparatively little pure mathematics, but a great deal of astronomy, cosmology, and biology.

With respect to the "primary" education Aristotle has a good deal to say. As "forcing" is always injurious, it should not be begun too soon. For the first five years a child's life should be given up to healthy play. Great care must be taken that children are not allowed to be too much with "servants," from whom they may imbibe low tastes, and that they are protected against any familiarity with indecency. From five to seven a child may begin to make a first easy acquaintance with the life of the school by looking on at the lessons of its elders. The real work of school education is to begin at seven and not before.

We next have to consider what should be the staple subjects of an education meant not for those who are to follow some particular calling, but for all the full citizens of a State. Aristotle's view is that some "useful" subjects must, of course, be taught. Reading and writing, for instance, are useful for the discharge of the business of life, though their commercial utility is not the highest value which they have for us. But care must be taken that only those "useful" studies which are also "liberal" should be taught; "illiberal" or "mechanical" subjects must not have any place in the curriculum. A "liberal" education means, as the name shows, one which will tend to make its recipient a "free man," and not a slave in body and soul. The mechanical crafts were felt by Aristotle to be illiberal because they leave a man no leisure to make the best of body and mind; practice of them sets a stamp on the body and narrows the mind's outlook. In principle, then, no study should form a subject of the universal curriculum if its only value is that it prepares a man for a profession followed as a means of making a living. General education, all-round training which aims at the development of body and mind for its own sake, must be kept free from the intrusion of everything which has a merely commercial value and tends to contract the mental vision. It is the same principle which we rightly employ ourselves when we maintain that a university education ought not to include specialisation on merely "technical" or "professional" studies. The useful subjects which have at the same time a higher value as contributing to the formation of taste and character and serving to elevate and refine the mind include, besides reading and writing, which render great literature accessible to us, bodily culture (the true object of which is not merely to make the body strong and hardy, but to develop the moral qualities of grace and courage), music, and drawing. Aristotle holds that the real reason for making children learn music is (1) that the artistic appreciation of really great music is one of the ways in which "leisure" may be worthily employed, and to appreciate music rightly we must have some personal training in musical execution; (2) that all art, and music in particular, has a direct influence on character.

Plato and Aristotle, though they differ on certain points of detail, are agreed that the influence of music on character, for good or bad, is enormous. Music, they say, is the most imitative of all the arts. The various rhythms, times, and scales imitate different tempers and emotional moods, and it is a fundamental law of our nature that we grow like what we take pleasure in seeing or having imitated or represented for us. Hence if we are early accustomed to take pleasure in the imitation of the manly, resolute, and orderly, these qualities will in time become part of our own nature. This is why right musical education is so important that Plato declared that the revolutionary spirit always makes its first appearance in innovations on established musical form.

There is, however, one important difference between the two philosophers which must be noted, because it concerns

Aristotle's chief contribution to the philosophy of fine art. Plato had in the *Republic* proposed to expel florid, languishing, or unduly exciting forms of music not only from the schoolroom, but from life altogether, on the ground of their unwholesome tendency to foster an unstable and morbid character in those who enjoy them. For the same reason he had proposed the entire suppression of tragic drama. Aristotle has a theory which is directly aimed against this overstrained Puritanism. He holds that the exciting and sensational art which would be very bad as daily food may be very useful as an occasional medicine for the soul. He would retain even the most sensational forms of music on account of what he calls their "purgative" value. In the same spirit he asserts that the function of tragedy, with its sensational representations of the calamities of its heroes, is "by the vehicle of fear and pity to purge our minds of those and similar emotions." The explanation of the theory is to be sought in the literal sense of the medical term "purgative." According to the medical view which we have already found influencing his ethical doctrine, health consists in the maintenance of an equality between the various ingredients of the body. Every now and again it happens that there arise superfluous accretions of some one ingredient, which are not carried away in the normal routine of bodily life. These give rise to serious derangement of function, and may permanently injure the working of the organism, unless they are removed in time by a medicine which acts as a purge, and clears the body of a superfluous accumulation. The same thing also happens in the life of the soul. So long as we are in good spiritual health our various feelings and emotional moods will be readily discharged in action, in the course of our daily life. But there is always the possibility of an excessive accumulation of emotional "moods" for which the routine of daily life does not provide an adequate discharge in action. Unless this tendency is checked we may contract dangerously morbid habits of soul. Thus we need some medicine for the soul against this danger, which may be to it what a purgative is to the body.

Now it was a well-known fact, observed in connection with some of the more extravagant religious cults, that persons suffering from an excess of religious frenzy might be cured homoeopathically, so to say, by artificially arousing the very emotion in question by the use of exciting music. Aristotle extends the principle by suggesting that in the artificial excitement aroused by violently stimulating music or in the transports of sympathetic apprehension and pity with which we follow the disasters of the stage-hero, we have a safe and ready means of ridding ourselves of morbid emotional strain which might otherwise have worked havoc with the efficient conduct of real life.

The great value of this defence of the occasional employment of sensation as a medicine for the soul is obvious. Unhappily it would seem to have so dominated Aristotle's thought on the functions of dramatic art as to blind him to what we are accustomed to think the nobler functions of tragedy. No book has had a more curious fate than the little manual for intending composers of tragedies which is all that remains to us of Aristotle's lectures on Poetry. This is not the place to tell the story of the way in which the great classical French playwrights, who hopelessly misunderstood the meaning of Aristotle's chief special directions, but quite correctly divined that his lectures were meant to be an actual *Vade Mecum* for the dramatist, deliberately constructed their masterpieces in absolute submission to regulations for which they had no better reasons than that they had once been given magisterially by an ancient Greek philosopher. But it may be worth while to remark that the worth of Aristotle's account of tragedy as art-criticism has probably been vastly overrated. From first to last the standpoint he assumes, in his verdicts on the great tragic poets, is that of the gallery. What he insists on all through, probably because he has the purgative effect of the play always in his mind, is a well-woven plot with plenty of melodramatic surprise in the incidents and a thoroughly sensational culmination in a scene of unrelieved catastrophe over which the spectator can have a good cry, and so get well "purged" of his superfluous emotion. It is clear from his repeated allusions that the play he admired above all others was the *King Oedipus* of Sophocles, but it is equally clear that he admired it not for the profound insight into human life and destiny or the deep sense of the mystery of things which some modern critics have found in it, but because its plot is the best and most startling detective story ever devised, and its finale a triumph of melodramatic horror.

INDEX

Academy, Platonic 8, 10, 11, 61, 62, 70, 71
accident (as a predication) 24
action (as a category) 23
ACTIVE INTELLIGENCE, THE 86ff
actus purus 49
affective life 78
aitia, aition 50
Alcmaeon of Crotona 62
Alexander of Aphrodisas 87
Alexander the Great 6, 9–11
Alphonse the Wise 68
alteration (as motion) 56
Amyntas III 8
analogy, inference by 29–30
analytics 21
angels 67
"animal spirits" 82, 83
animals, perfect and imperfect 74
Antipater 11
Apollo Lyceus 10
appetition 58, 78–9, 97
Archidamian war 7
aristocracy 103–4

Aristotle
  life 6ff
  limitations of outlook 7
  provincialism 7
  will 12
  works 12ff, see also *Poetics*
art
  Art contrasted with Nature 63
  industrial and technical arts 16
  philosophy of art 20–1
  study of arts 108
Asclepiadae 8
assimilation (in sense-perception) 79–80
astronomy
  astronomy of A 61ff
  mediaeval astronomy 67–9
Atarneus in Aeolis 8
augmentation (as motion) 56
axioms 35–6

Bacon, Francis 6, 29, 62
balance 94–5
"barbarians" 7, 102

113

being, modes of   42
BIOLOGY   74ff
body and mind, doctrine of   76
Brasidas   7
Burnet, Professor   95

Callisthenes   11
categories of propositions   22, 24
causation, theory of   51
cause
    classification of causes   50
    efficient cause   50, 55, 74, 96
    the four causes   50ff
Chalcidic federation   7
Chalcis   6, 11
chance   53-4
character   92
Cicero   12-13, 83-4
CLASSIFICATION OF THE SCIENCES:
    SCIENTIFIC METHOD, THE   14ff
CLASSIFICATION OF THE SCIENCES
    15ff
cognition   78
"common sense"   83
COMMON SENSIBLES AND THE
    COMMON SENSE-ORGAN, THE
    81ff
common sensorium   82, 83
community   100-1
conation   78
condition (as a category)   23
consciousness   75
constitutional government   105
Constitution of Athens, A's essay
    on   13
CONTINUOUS MOTION AND THE
    "SPHERES"   66ff
contradiction, law of   40, 41
Copernican hypothesis   61
Corinth   7
Creationism   56

Dante   6, 54, 67, 68, 70, 73, 78, 87
Darwin   61
decay (as motion)   56
definition
    definition as predication   24-6
    definition as a process   46
    nominal and real definition   27
democracy   103
Demosthenes   6
Descartes   5, 75
dialectic
    function of dialectic   15, 17
    dialectic reasoning   40
difference (as predication)   24
diminution (as motion)   56
Discourses of Socrates (Plato)   12
Discourses on Conduct   13
dream-life   83

eccentrics   68
economics   17, 20
education   45, 76, 90, 92-4, 101,
    105ff
eidos   44
elements
    elements and compounds   63
    elements of Empedocles   46,
    61-2, 71
Empedocles   46, 71
empiricism   38, 85
energeia   49
entelechy   49, 76
epicycles   68
epistemology   32
ETERNITY OF MOTION, THE   56ff
Ethics, or Discourses on Conduct   9,
    13, 20, 49, 90, 99
ethics   16, 20, see also Ethics
Euboea   6
Euclid   35, 45
Eudaimonia   90

Eudemian Ethics 13
Eudemus 13
Eudoxus of Cnidus 69
evolution
    ancient evolution 56
    modern evolutionary science 26

family 100, 101
fantasy 83
females 51
"fifth body" 70
"first moved" 66ff
FIRST PHILOSOPHY 41ff
"Five Words" 22, 23, 24
FORMAL LOGIC 21ff
form and matter 43, 44ff
FOUR CAUSES, THE 50ff

Galileo 6, 69–70
generation
    generation as motion 55
    "aequivocal generation" 74
genus (as predication) 24
God 18, 52, 57ff, 66, 87, 99, see
    also Nature
Goethe 72
golden mean 6
goodness 92–8
Good, On the 9
GRADES OF PHYSICAL LIFE 77ff
gravity 72

happiness 90–1
heart 82–3
heaven 64
Hegel 14, 38
Hermeias 8, 9, 11
Herpyllis 12
Hipparchus 69
Hippocrates 62
Hudibras quotation 47

hybrids 53
hyle 44

Ibn Roshd 87
idealism
    idealism of A 47
    idealism of Plato 31–2
ideas (see also THOUGHT)
    A's view of thought 33ff
    "innate thought" 85
    Plato's doctrine of thought 32
imagery 83–4
INDUCTION 29ff, also 34, 37–8
inference, doctrine of 27
"informed" mind 84–5
intelligence
    A's conception of intelligence 85
    active intelligence 86ff
    intelligence as efficient cause 53
Isocrates 9

Kant 5, 82
kind, differences of 25–6
kinesis 54
knowledge
    intuitive knowledge 35, 36–9
    theory of knowledge 30ff

leisure 99
liberal education 6, 105, 107
life
    affective life 78
    psychical life 77ff
    stages of life 77
LIFE AND WORKS 5ff
Life of Alexander (Plutarch) 9
LIFE OF ARISTOTLE 6ff
locomotion 78
logic 21ff
Lotze 55
Lyceum 10, 11

Marcus Aurelius 62
mathematics 18
MATTER AND FORM 44ff, also 43
matter (see also MATTER AND FORM)
  kinds of matter 70
  qualitative differences in matter
   71
means and ends 89
mediaeval
  mediaeval astronomy 67–9
  mediaeval ethics 54
  mediaeval logic 24
  mediaeval theology 87
medicine 16
memory, theory of 83
Metaphysica 18
metaphysics 18
METHODS OF SCIENCE 21ff
middle term 35
military training 106
Mill, John Stuart 30, 37, 38, 52
Milton 6, 68, 69
monarchy 103
MOTION 54ff
motion (see also MOTION)
  continuous motion 66ff
  eternity of motion 56ff
  motion through space 56
  planetary motion 67
  varieties of motion 55–6
music 108

Nature
  A's conception of Nature 63
  God and Nature 52
  Nature as efficient cause 53
Nicomachean Ethics 13
Nicomachus (father) 8
Nicomachus (son) 12, 13
nominalism 25–7
notiora naturae 34

Oedipus, King (Sophocles) 111
oligarchy 103
On the Good 9
"opposites" 72
Organon 21
organ, the central 81–2

passivity (as a category) 23
Pericles 7, 104
Peripatetic 10
Phaedo 60
Philip of Macedon 7, 9, 10
philsophy
  A's conception of philosophy
   14, 84
  first philosophy 18, 19, 27, 41ff
  practical philosophy 20, 88ff
  productive philosophy 20
  "synthetic philosophy" 47
PHYSICS 61ff, also 18, 19
place (as category) 23
Plato 12, 13, 17, 23, 30–3, 39, 45,
  59, 60, 61–2, 69, 72–3, 81, 90,
  93, 96, 106, 108–9, see also
  Academy, Platonic
Plotinus 75
Plutarch 9
Poetics 20, 110–11
poetry, A's lectures on 110
points 65
Politics 9, 21, 88, 99, 103–5
politics (see also *Politics*)
  A's conception of politics
   89–90
  science of politics 16, 17, 20
polity 105
Porphyry 24
postulates 35
POTENTIAL AND THE ACTUAL, THE
  48ff, also 43, 81, 85
PRACTICAL PHILOSOPHY 88ff

predicables 22
predicaments 22
predication 43
primary education 107
primum mobile 66ff
principles
    principles of science 39, 41
    self-evident principles 17
probablism 15
"proper place" 73
property (as a category) 23–4, 25
propositions, doctrine of 27
proprium, see property
psyche 75
psychical life 77ff
PSYCHOLOGY 75ff
Ptolemy 69
"purgative" (of art) 109
Pythagoras 45
Pythagoreans 61–2
Pythias 8, 12

quality
    quality as a category 22
    quality of a proposition 27
quantity
    quantity as a category 22
    quantity of a proposition 27
quintessence 71

relation (as a category) 22
Republic (Plato) 109
rhetoric 20
rhetorical reasoning 30
"right proportion" 80
rotation 56

scholasticism 57, 87
schoolmen 40
science
    A's conception of science 15,
    86

diagrammatic classification of
    sciences 19
methods of science 21ff
principle of science 39, 41
special sciences 41
speculative and practical sciences
    16
self-consciousness 75, 82
SENSATION 78ff
sense-perception 79, 82
sexual reproduction 74
slavery 102
Socrates 11, 12, 29, 60
Sophistry 15, 16
Sophocles 5, 111
soul 75–6
space 64–5
Sparta 7
Speusippus 8, 10
"spheres" 67
"spiritual" doctrine 96
spontaneity 63
state (as a category) 23
state, theory of (political) 100ff
Stoics 22, 84
St. Thomas (Aquinus) 40, 57, 60,
    75, 87
substance 22, 42–3, see also TER-
    RESTRIAL BODIES
Summa Theologiae (St. Thomas)
    40
syllogism
    A's treatment of syllogism 22,
    27–8
    figures of syllogism 28
    middle term of syllogism 35
    syllogism of action 98

terms, doctrine of 22
TERRESTRIAL BODIES 71ff
Thackeray 104

theology 18, 55, 87
THEORY OF KNOWLEDGE 30ff
THEORY OF THE STATE, THE
 100ff
THOUGHT 84ff
time
 nature of time 65
 perception of time 82
 time as a category 23
tragic drama 109
"transcendental moonshine" 30,
 39
transference 56
transmutation 71–2
"trepidation" 69

understanding 85
universal truths 17

vacuum 72
vita contemplativa, vita activa 100
volition 17

weight, doctrine of 72ff
Weimar 104
will 94, 96–7
wisdom 97–8
WORKS OF ARISTOTLE 12ff
wrong-doing 96–7

Xenocrates of Chalcedon 10

A CATALOGUE OF SELECTED DOVER BOOKS
IN ALL FIELDS OF INTEREST

A CATALOGUE OF SELECTED DOVER BOOKS
IN ALL FIELDS OF INTEREST

AMERICA'S OLD MASTERS, James T. Flexner. Four men emerged unexpectedly from provincial 18th century America to leadership in European art: Benjamin West, J. S. Copley, C. R. Peale, Gilbert Stuart. Brilliant coverage of lives and contributions. Revised, 1967 edition. 69 plates. 365pp. of text.

21806-6 Paperbound $3.00

FIRST FLOWERS OF OUR WILDERNESS: AMERICAN PAINTING, THE COLONIAL PERIOD, James T. Flexner. Painters, and regional painting traditions from earliest Colonial times up to the emergence of Copley, West and Peale Sr., Foster, Gustavus Hesselius, Feke, John Smibert and many anonymous painters in the primitive manner. Engaging presentation, with 162 illustrations. xxii + 368pp.

22180-6 Paperbound $3.50

THE LIGHT OF DISTANT SKIES: AMERICAN PAINTING, 1760-1835, James T. Flexner. The great generation of early American painters goes to Europe to learn and to teach: West, Copley, Gilbert Stuart and others. Allston, Trumbull, Morse; also contemporary American painters—primitives, derivatives, academics—who remained in America. 102 illustrations. xiii + 306pp.

22179-2 Paperbound $3.00

A HISTORY OF THE RISE AND PROGRESS OF THE ARTS OF DESIGN IN THE UNITED STATES, William Dunlap. Much the richest mine of information on early American painters, sculptors, architects, engravers, miniaturists, etc. The only source of information for scores of artists, the major primary source for many others. Unabridged reprint of rare original 1834 edition, with new introduction by James T. Flexner, and 394 new illustrations. Edited by Rita Weiss. 6⅝ x 9⅝.

21695-0, 21696-9, 21697-7 Three volumes, Paperbound $13.50

EPOCHS OF CHINESE AND JAPANESE ART, Ernest F. Fenollosa. From primitive Chinese art to the 20th century, thorough history, explanation of every important art period and form, including Japanese woodcuts; main stress on China and Japan, but Tibet, Korea also included. Still unexcelled for its detailed, rich coverage of cultural background, aesthetic elements, diffusion studies, particularly of the historical period. 2nd, 1913 edition. 242 illustrations. lii + 439pp. of text.

20364-6, 20365-4 Two volumes, Paperbound $6.00

THE GENTLE ART OF MAKING ENEMIES, James A. M. Whistler. Greatest wit of his day deflates Oscar Wilde, Ruskin, Swinburne; strikes back at inane critics, exhibitions, art journalism; aesthetics of impressionist revolution in most striking form. Highly readable classic by great painter. Reproduction of edition designed by Whistler. Introduction by Alfred Werner. xxxvi + 334pp.

21875-9 Paperbound $2.50

EAST O' THE SUN AND WEST O' THE MOON, George W. Dasent. Considered the best of all translations of these Norwegian folk tales, this collection has been enjoyed by generations of children (and folklorists too). Includes True and Untrue, Why the Sea is Salt, East O' the Sun and West O' the Moon, Why the Bear is Stumpy-Tailed, Boots and the Troll, The Cock and the Hen, Rich Peter the Pedlar, and 52 more. The only edition with all 59 tales. 77 illustrations by Erik Werenskiold and Theodor Kittelsen. xv + 418pp. 22521-6 Paperbound $3.50

GOOPS AND HOW TO BE THEM, Gelett Burgess. Classic of tongue-in-cheek humor, masquerading as etiquette book. 87 verses, twice as many cartoons, show mischievous Goops as they demonstrate to children virtues of table manners, neatness, courtesy, etc. Favorite for generations. viii + 88pp. 6½ x 9¼. 22233-0 Paperbound $1.25

ALICE'S ADVENTURES UNDER GROUND, Lewis Carroll. The first version, quite different from the final *Alice in Wonderland,* printed out by Carroll himself with his own illustrations. Complete facsimile of the "million dollar" manuscript Carroll gave to Alice Liddell in 1864. Introduction by Martin Gardner. viii + 96pp. Title and dedication pages in color. 21482-6 Paperbound $1.25

THE BROWNIES, THEIR BOOK, Palmer Cox. Small as mice, cunning as foxes, exuberant and full of mischief, the Brownies go to the zoo, toy shop, seashore, circus, etc., in 24 verse adventures and 266 illustrations. Long a favorite, since their first appearance in St. Nicholas Magazine. xi + 144pp. 6⅝ x 9¼. 21265-3 Paperbound $1.75

SONGS OF CHILDHOOD, Walter De La Mare. Published (under the pseudonym Walter Ramal) when De La Mare was only 29, this charming collection has long been a favorite children's book. A facsimile of the first edition in paper, the 47 poems capture the simplicity of the nursery rhyme and the ballad, including such lyrics as I Met Eve, Tartary, The Silver Penny. vii + 106pp. 21972-0 Paperbound $1.25

THE COMPLETE NONSENSE OF EDWARD LEAR, Edward Lear. The finest 19th-century humorist-cartoonist in full: all nonsense limericks, zany alphabets, Owl and Pussycat, songs, nonsense botany, and more than 500 illustrations by Lear himself. Edited by Holbrook Jackson. xxix + 287pp. (USO) 20167-8 Paperbound $2.00

BILLY WHISKERS: THE AUTOBIOGRAPHY OF A GOAT, Frances Trego Montgomery. A favorite of children since the early 20th century, here are the escapades of that rambunctious, irresistible and mischievous goat—Billy Whiskers. Much in the spirit of *Peck's Bad Boy,* this is a book that children never tire of reading or hearing. All the original familiar illustrations by W. H. Fry are included: 6 color plates, 18 black and white drawings. 159pp. 22345-0 Paperbound $2.00

MOTHER GOOSE MELODIES. Faithful republication of the fabulously rare Munroe and Francis "copyright 1833" Boston edition—the most important Mother Goose collection, usually referred to as the "original." Familiar rhymes plus many rare ones, with wonderful old woodcut illustrations. Edited by E. F. Bleiler. 128pp. 4½ x 6⅜. 22577-1 Paperbound $1.25

POEMS OF ANNE BRADSTREET, edited with an introduction by Robert Hutchinson. A new selection of poems by America's first poet and perhaps the first significant woman poet in the English language. 48 poems display her development in works of considerable variety—love poems, domestic poems, religious meditations, formal elegies, "quaternions," etc. Notes, bibliography. viii + 222pp.

22160-1 Paperbound $2.00

THREE GOTHIC NOVELS: THE CASTLE OF OTRANTO BY HORACE WALPOLE; VATHEK BY WILLIAM BECKFORD; THE VAMPYRE BY JOHN POLIDORI, WITH FRAGMENT OF A NOVEL BY LORD BYRON, edited by E. F. Bleiler. The first Gothic novel, by Walpole; the finest Oriental tale in English, by Beckford; powerful Romantic supernatural story in versions by Polidori and Byron. All extremely important in history of literature; all still exciting, packed with supernatural thrills, ghosts, haunted castles, magic, etc. xl + 291pp.

21232-7 Paperbound $2.50

THE BEST TALES OF HOFFMANN, E. T. A. Hoffmann. 10 of Hoffmann's most important stories, in modern re-editings of standard translations: Nutcracker and the King of Mice, Signor Formica, Automata, The Sandman, Rath Krespel, The Golden Flowerpot, Master Martin the Cooper, The Mines of Falun, The King's Betrothed, A New Year's Eve Adventure. 7 illustrations by Hoffmann. Edited by E. F. Bleiler. xxxix + 419pp. 21793-0 Paperbound $3.00

GHOST AND HORROR STORIES OF AMBROSE BIERCE, Ambrose Bierce. 23 strikingly modern stories of the horrors latent in the human mind: The Eyes of the Panther, The Damned Thing, An Occurrence at Owl Creek Bridge, An Inhabitant of Carcosa, etc., plus the dream-essay, Visions of the Night. Edited by E. F. Bleiler. xxii + 199pp. 20767-6 Paperbound $1.50

BEST GHOST STORIES OF J. S. LEFANU, J. Sheridan LeFanu. Finest stories by Victorian master often considered greatest supernatural writer of all. Carmilla, Green Tea, The Haunted Baronet, The Familiar, and 12 others. Most never before available in the U. S. A. Edited by E. F. Bleiler. 8 illustrations from Victorian publications. xvii + 467pp. 20415-4 Paperbound $3.00

MATHEMATICAL FOUNDATIONS OF INFORMATION THEORY, A. I. Khinchin. Comprehensive introduction to work of Shannon, McMillan, Feinstein and Khinchin, placing these investigations on a rigorous mathematical basis. Covers entropy concept in probability theory, uniqueness theorem, Shannon's inequality, ergodic sources, the E property, martingale concept, noise, Feinstein's fundamental lemma, Shanon's first and second theorems. Translated by R. A. Silverman and M. D. Friedman. iii + 120pp. 60434-9 Paperbound $1.75

SEVEN SCIENCE FICTION NOVELS, H. G. Wells. The standard collection of the great novels. Complete, unabridged. *First Men in the Moon, Island of Dr. Moreau, War of the Worlds, Food of the Gods, Invisible Man, Time Machine, In the Days of the Comet.* Not only science fiction fans, but every educated person owes it to himself to read these novels. 1015pp 20264-X Clothbound $5.00

DESIGN BY ACCIDENT; A BOOK OF "ACCIDENTAL EFFECTS" FOR ARTISTS AND DESIGNERS, James F. O'Brien. Create your own unique, striking, imaginative effects by "controlled accident" interaction of materials: paints and lacquers, oil and water based paints, splatter, crackling materials, shatter, similar items. Everything you do will be different; first book on this limitless art, so useful to both fine artist and commercial artist. Full instructions. 192 plates showing "accidents," 8 in color. viii + 215pp. 8⅜ x 11¼.   21942-9 Paperbound $3.50

THE BOOK OF SIGNS, Rudolf Koch. Famed German type designer draws 493 beautiful symbols: religious, mystical, alchemical, imperial, property marks, runes, etc. Remarkable fusion of traditional and modern. Good for suggestions of timelessness, smartness, modernity. Text. vi + 104pp. 6⅛ x 9¼.
                              20162-7 Paperbound $1.25

HISTORY OF INDIAN AND INDONESIAN ART, Ananda K. Coomaraswamy. An unabridged republication of one of the finest books by a great scholar in Eastern art. Rich in descriptive material, history, social backgrounds; Sunga reliefs, Rajput paintings, Gupta temples, Burmese frescoes, textiles, jewelry, sculpture, etc. 400 photos. viii + 423pp. 6⅜ x 9¾.   21436-2 Paperbound $4.00

PRIMITIVE ART, Franz Boas. America's foremost anthropologist surveys textiles, ceramics, woodcarving, basketry, metalwork, etc.; patterns, technology, creation of symbols, style origins. All areas of world, but very full on Northwest Coast Indians. More than 350 illustrations of baskets, boxes, totem poles, weapons, etc. 378 pp.
                              20025-6 Paperbound $3.00

THE GENTLEMAN AND CABINET MAKER'S DIRECTOR, Thomas Chippendale. Full reprint (third edition, 1762) of most influential furniture book of all time, by master cabinetmaker. 200 plates, illustrating chairs, sofas, mirrors, tables, cabinets, plus 24 photographs of surviving pieces. Biographical introduction by N. Bienenstock. vi + 249pp. 9⅞ x 12¾.   21601-2 Paperbound $4.00

AMERICAN ANTIQUE FURNITURE, Edgar G. Miller, Jr. The basic coverage of all American furniture before 1840. Individual chapters cover type of furniture—clocks, tables, sideboards, etc.—chronologically, with inexhaustible wealth of data. More than 2100 photographs, all identified, commented on. Essential to all early American collectors. Introduction by H. E. Keyes. vi + 1106pp. 7⅞ x 10¾.
                    21599-7, 21600-4 Two volumes, Paperbound $11.00

PENNSYLVANIA DUTCH AMERICAN FOLK ART, Henry J. Kauffman. 279 photos, 28 drawings of tulipware, Fraktur script, painted tinware, toys, flowered furniture, quilts, samplers, hex signs, house interiors, etc. Full descriptive text. Excellent for tourist, rewarding for designer, collector. Map. 146pp. 7⅞ x 10¾.
                              21205-X Paperbound $2.50

EARLY NEW ENGLAND GRAVESTONE RUBBINGS, Edmund V. Gillon, Jr. 43 photographs, 226 carefully reproduced rubbings show heavily symbolic, sometimes macabre early gravestones, up to early 19th century. Remarkable early American primitive art, occasionally strikingly beautiful; always powerful. Text. xxvi + 207pp. 8⅜ x 11¼.   21380-3 Paperbound $3.50

THE ARCHITECTURE OF COUNTRY HOUSES, Andrew J. Downing. Together with Vaux's *Villas and Cottages* this is the basic book for Hudson River Gothic architecture of the middle Victorian period. Full, sound discussions of general aspects of housing, architecture, style, decoration, furnishing, together with scores of detailed house plans, illustrations of specific buildings, accompanied by full text. Perhaps the most influential single American architectural book. 1850 edition. Introduction by J. Stewart Johnson. 321 figures, 34 architectural designs. xvi + 560pp.

22003-6 Paperbound $4.00

LOST EXAMPLES OF COLONIAL ARCHITECTURE, John Mead Howells. Full-page photographs of buildings that have disappeared or been so altered as to be denatured, including many designed by major early American architects. 245 plates. xvii + 248pp. 7⅞ x 10¾.

21143-6 Paperbound $3.50

DOMESTIC ARCHITECTURE OF THE AMERICAN COLONIES AND OF THE EARLY REPUBLIC, Fiske Kimball. Foremost architect and restorer of Williamsburg and Monticello covers nearly 200 homes between 1620-1825. Architectural details, construction, style features, special fixtures, floor plans, etc. Generally considered finest work in its area. 219 illustrations of houses, doorways, windows, capital mantels. xx + 314pp. 7⅞ x 10¾.

21743-4 Paperbound $4.00

EARLY AMERICAN ROOMS: 1650-1858, edited by Russell Hawes Kettell. Tour of 12 rooms, each representative of a different era in American history and each furnished, decorated, designed and occupied in the style of the era. 72 plans and elevations, 8-page color section, etc., show fabrics, wall papers, arrangements, etc. Full descriptive text. xvii + 200pp. of text. 8⅜ x 11¼.

21633-0 Paperbound $5.00

THE FITZWILLIAM VIRGINAL BOOK, edited by J. Fuller Maitland and W. B. Squire. Full modern printing of famous early 17th-century ms. volume of 300 works by Morley, Byrd, Bull, Gibbons, etc. For piano or other modern keyboard instrument; easy to read format. xxxvi + 938pp. 8⅜ x 11.

21068-5, 21069-3 Two volumes, Paperbound $10.00

KEYBOARD MUSIC, Johann Sebastian Bach. Bach Gesellschaft edition. A rich selection of Bach's masterpieces for the harpsichord: the six English Suites, six French Suites, the six Partitas (Clavierübung part I), the Goldberg Variations (Clavierübung part IV), the fifteen Two-Part Inventions and the fifteen Three-Part Sinfonias. Clearly reproduced on large sheets with ample margins; eminently playable. vi + 312pp. 8⅛ x 11.

22360-4 Paperbound $5.00

THE MUSIC OF BACH: AN INTRODUCTION, Charles Sanford Terry. A fine, nontechnical introduction to Bach's music, both instrumental and vocal. Covers organ music, chamber music, passion music, other types. Analyzes themes, developments, innovations. x + 114pp.

21075-8 Paperbound $1.25

BEETHOVEN AND HIS NINE SYMPHONIES, Sir George Grove. Noted British musicologist provides best history, analysis, commentary on symphonies. Very thorough, rigorously accurate; necessary to both advanced student and amateur music lover. 436 musical passages. vii + 407 pp.

20334-4 Paperbound $2.75

MATHEMATICAL PUZZLES FOR BEGINNERS AND ENTHUSIASTS, Geoffrey Mott-Smith. 189 puzzles from easy to difficult—involving arithmetic, logic, algebra, properties of digits, probability, etc.—for enjoyment and mental stimulus. Explanation of mathematical principles behind the puzzles. 135 illustrations. viii + 248pp.

20198-8 Paperbound $1.75

PAPER FOLDING FOR BEGINNERS, William D. Murray and Francis J. Rigney. Easiest book on the market, clearest instructions on making interesting, beautiful origami. Sail boats, cups, roosters, frogs that move legs, bonbon boxes, standing birds, etc. 40 projects; more than 275 diagrams and photographs. 94pp.

20713-7 Paperbound $1.00

TRICKS AND GAMES ON THE POOL TABLE, Fred Herrmann. 79 tricks and games—some solitaires, some for two or more players, some competitive games—to entertain you between formal games. Mystifying shots and throws, unusual caroms, tricks involving such props as cork, coins, a hat, etc. Formerly *Fun on the Pool Table*. 77 figures. 95pp.

21814-7 Paperbound $1.00

HAND SHADOWS TO BE THROWN UPON THE WALL: A SERIES OF NOVEL AND AMUSING FIGURES FORMED BY THE HAND, Henry Bursill. Delightful picturebook from great-grandfather's day shows how to make 18 different hand shadows: a bird that flies, duck that quacks, dog that wags his tail, camel, goose, deer, boy, turtle, etc. Only book of its sort. vi + 33pp. 6½ x 9¼. 21779-5 Paperbound $1.00

WHITTLING AND WOODCARVING, E. J. Tangerman. 18th printing of best book on market. "If you can cut a potato you can carve" toys and puzzles, chains, chessmen, caricatures, masks, frames, woodcut blocks, surface patterns, much more. Information on tools, woods, techniques. Also goes into serious wood sculpture from Middle Ages to present, East and West. 464 photos, figures. x + 293pp.

20965-2 Paperbound $2.00

HISTORY OF PHILOSOPHY, Julián Marias. Possibly the clearest, most easily followed, best planned, most useful one-volume history of philosophy on the market; neither skimpy nor overfull. Full details on system of every major philosopher and dozens of less important thinkers from pre-Socratics up to Existentialism and later. Strong on many European figures usually omitted. Has gone through dozens of editions in Europe. 1966 edition, translated by Stanley Appelbaum and Clarence Strowbridge. xviii + 505pp. 21739-6 Paperbound $3.00

YOGA: A SCIENTIFIC EVALUATION, Kovoor T. Behanan. Scientific but non-technical study of physiological results of yoga exercises; done under auspices of Yale U. Relations to Indian thought, to psychoanalysis, etc. 16 photos. xxiii + 270pp.

20505-3 Paperbound $2.50